REVOLUTIONARY
IMMORTALITY

REVOLUTIONARY IMMORTALITY

MAO TSE-TUNG
AND THE CHINESE
CULTURAL REVOLUTION

BY Robert Jay Lifton

 Random House · New York

The author wishes to thank the following for permission to quote material which appears in this volume:
Simon and Schuster, Inc., for *Mao Tse-Tung*, by Stuart Schram. Copyright © 1966 by Stuart Schram.
Random House, Inc., for *The China Reader: Communist China*, edited by Franz Schurmann and Orville Schell. Copyright © 1967 by Franz Schurmann and Orville Schell. Copyright © 1966 by Franz Schurmann.

May the Revolutionary Regime stay Red
for ten thousand generations.

—CHINESE COMMUNIST SLOGAN

As long as we are not assured of immortality,
we shall never be fulfilled, we shall go on hating
each other in spite of our need for mutual love.

—EUGENE IONESCO

REVOLUTIONARY
IMMORTALITY

Preface

Books are responses to events. The unusual events in China from mid-1966 through early 1968 have led me to attempt a rather unusual kind of book. It is about Mao Tse-tung and the Cultural Revolution, but its larger concern is with men's efforts to render their works, and especially their revolutionary works, eternal. It is therefore a study of the vicissitudes of human continuity.

The book evolves from a long-standing general interest in the contemporary interplay of psychology and history, as well as a specific interest in Communist China's unique efforts at remaking men and women according to her ideological vision. My earlier study, *Thought Reform and the Psychology of Totalism,* explored these efforts as they extended into the late 1950s, including the "Hundred Flowers" episode of 1956–1957 and its aftermath. During the early 1960s my research interests turned to Japan, but I continued to follow events on the mainland as closely as I could. Once one has immersed oneself in matters Chinese, one never quite extricates oneself from them, nor does one wish to.

Until about the beginning of 1966, although much of great interest continued to take place in China, I had the impression that events were generally consistent with the patterns of reform or "rectification," followed by relative liberalization, that I had previously observed. During the late spring and early summer of 1966, however, this suddenly ceased to be true. Reports were confused, but they left no doubt that a movement of a very different order was developing. I found myself, like many others, puzzled and fascinated as I followed the Cultural Revolution from New Haven, New York, Cape Cod, and then London. My earlier work had provided many possible leads, but these seemed if anything to deepen the mystery. At that time a new English edition of my book on thought reform was being scheduled, and the publisher's suggestion that I add a brief section on the Cultural Revolution seemed to me both sensible and problematic. Fortunately I was soon to be on my way to the Far East for a half year of follow-up interviews with young Japanese, and in February 1967 I was able to arrange a brief stay in Hong Kong for the purpose of gaining a closer glimpse of mainland events.

The Hong Kong re-exposure (I had done my original work there in 1954–1955, and had returned for shorter visits on two subsequent occasions) was invaluable. There I could gather a great variety of extremely useful materials, and at the same time exchange impressions with a large number of China-watchers who were thinking, talking about, and imbibing nothing but the Cultural Revolution. I could also converse at length with a few Westerners and Chinese who had recently come from the mainland, including one young man who had been actively involved in the Red Guard movement. I was thus able to obtain a "feel" of the Cultural Revolution—a sense of the extraordinary environment that had been created in China and of the forces contributing to that environment.

I became increasingly aware that the general psychological principles governing the thought reform process could not adequately illuminate the Cultural Revolution. Its agitated extremities of destruction and attempted revitalization demanded a larger perspective, one that could deal with man's struggles for various forms of renewal and transcendence. I had been thinking about such a perspective for some time in relationship to other work. Partly from research in Hiroshima, but also from a continuing effort to formulate the nature of the individual experience in historical change, I had evolved a series of concepts around what I call modes of symbolic immortality. These deal with both death symbolism and human continuity, and in a work in progress I had begun to apply them to different epochs and to a general view of the historical process.

The approach is consistent with Otto Rank's emphasis upon man's continuing need for "an assurance of eternal survival for his self." But while Rank saw this need as part of man's "irrational" nature, it seemed to me best understood as an aspect of his symbolic life, which in itself is neither "rational" nor "irrational" but comprehensible within a formal and (in the larger meaning of the word) scientific framework. The *sense* of immortality, then, is the individual's connection with man's general past and future. I found the concept of symbolic immortality to be highly relevant to the issues of personal and historical continuity, and to related matters of ideological purity, dominating the Cultural Revolution. What seemed indicated was a careful exploration, in the light of this concept, of forces at play in that movement. But this kind of exploration had to take on its own autonomy, had to become at the very least a "slim volume."

In Tokyo during the spring of 1967 I worked with some excitement on the first draft of the manuscript. It was a good place to do so, for Japanese reporters and travelers were moving more freely among the participants in the Cultural Revolution (then still in full swing) than were their Western counterparts. They were also better able to read the wall posters (even if they occasionally made mistakes); and in their reports—as well as in our conversations—they conveyed perhaps better than any other group a vivid sense of the movement's evangelical enthusiasm and zealotry. Once I was back in the United States I had opportunities to present the general argument of the book, first to a summer work group devoted to "psychohistorical" problems, and then to a Yale audience of faculty and students in Chinese Studies. The responses evoked strengthened my belief that this unconventional approach could have significance for a variety of people coming to the subject from very different vantage points.

What has emerged is an interpretive essay whose central theme—that of revolutionary immortality—serves to organize a large number of divergent events and attitudes. I want to stress that this is by no means the only theme one could have chosen for such a purpose. One could have instead emphasized the economic strains of a developing country, China's confrontation with America, the Sino-Soviet dispute, or the inevitable conflicts arising in the history of any revolution. Large historical events cannot be attributed to a single cause, nor grasped by a single explanation.

Neither is mine the only possible psychological approach. One could have stressed, for instance, Mao's individual-psychological development in more usual psychoanalytic terms, with emphasis upon the monumental conflict with his father which all accounts suggest. Indeed, a full-scale psychobiography of Mao will surely be undertaken sometime in the future, but that is not my intention here. Rather, I focus upon certain features of Mao's psychological and revolutionary style as these come to bear upon a series of personal and historical exigencies of his and China's situation. Such a focus is part of a continuing effort to find new conceptual connections between individual and collective patterns, especially under extreme historical conditions. What I would claim for the use of the theme of symbolic immortality is a particular pertinence to this kind of extreme episode, and a general inclusiveness permitting the alternative themes mentioned earlier to be taken into account.

It enables me, for instance, to explore, in what I believe to be a new way, an excruciatingly complex encounter between man and technology. While rejecting the simple polarity of rational versus irrational behavior, I have found it necessary here to make certain psychological judgments concerning attitudes and behavior as they relate to the potentialities of the environment. One example is the concept of "psychism," the exaggerated reliance upon will and psychic power to achieve technological goals. But I apply the concept only where there have been strong indications of this tendency, as confirmed by peculiarly self-defeating results.

The evidence I cite does not derive from the kind of systematic series of interviews I have done in connection with previous work. I did conduct a number of interviews and found them extremely informative. But I also depend upon observations at a distance—upon writings and reported actions of Mao and others—and I do not hesitate to speculate about the relationship of these to the general themes I develop. I do, however, attempt to discipline this speculation both by seeking converging evidence from several directions and by making explicit the steps of my psychological argument. Above all I stress shared experience and avoid resorting to what I regard as a solipsistic tendency all too common in my own profession, that of viewing large historical events as nothing but manifestations of someone's individual psychopathology. I have in fact become newly impressed by the potential usefulness of a category of data falling somewhere between group ideology and individual-psychological style—a level of experience that has been largely ignored but which, I believe, will take on considerable future importance for both psychologists and historians.

I confine myself to the Chinese Cultural Revolution, preferring to leave farther-ranging theoretical explorations for another study. But as my title implies, I see the Chinese situation as a paradigm for revolutions in general. Hence, I believe that the experience of the Soviet Union could be profitably re-examined in relationship to the theme of revolutionary immortality—focusing upon the early expression of the Marxist–Leninist vision, and viewing subsequent developments under Stalin, Khrushchev, and the present regime as embodying simultaneous attempts to eternalize and alter that vision. One could bring a similar approach to the French Revolution, and to a number of other partial or even failed revolutions. Not that these events are all the same: indeed, the framework I suggest might shed some light on why one revolution aborts at its inception, another changes the world, and a third succeeds and then consumes itself.

To generalize in this way does not preclude, and in fact requires, a stress upon what is peculiarly Chinese. Only from an emphasis upon cultural roots and historical context can one derive the stuff of generalization. An upheaval like the Cultural Revolution demonstrates all too forcibly the need to view Chinese behavior neither as identical in motivation and nuance with Western behavior, nor as a self-enclosed form of Oriental exoticism. To see Chinese experience as both distinctive and part of the general flow of human events would seem a simple enough principle, but it has been long in coming into practice. China differentiates herself from the West by means of her specific combination of cultural symbols evolved over the course of her history. But these symbols depend upon psychobiological potential available to all men in all epochs; they are, moreover, subject to the increasingly shared currents of world history.

Finally, I hope that this essay speaks to certain contemporary issues quite beyond China's struggles or even general questions of revolution. I refer to dilemmas of historical discontinuity—to the broken connection or impaired sense of immortality—that now affect people in every society. By gaining some understanding of China's resulting combination of desperation and excess we may better learn to live not only with her but with ourselves as well. My hope in fact is that this study of a closed and totalistic revolutionary vision will serve to strengthen the more humane and searching forms of radical thought now struggling to take shape throughout the world, especially among the young.

My debts in this work are many, but I will mention only a few of them: enlarging dialogues over the years with Erik H. Erikson, David Riesman, and Kenneth Keniston; continuing mentorship on matters Chinese from Benjamin I. Schwartz, John K. Fairbank, Mary C. Wright, and Arthur F. Wright; thoughtful responses to the manuscript from all of the above, as well as from Jonathan D. Spence, Lawrence W. Chisolm, and Frederick C. Redlich; valuable suggestions from members of the Group for the Study of Psychohistorical Process; generous help with references and Chinese terminology from Weiying Wan; careful preparation of the manuscript by Lily B. Finn; and much of everything from my wife, Betty Jean Lifton.

R. J. L.
New Haven, Connecticut
March, 1968

Contents

I

THE "POWER STRUGGLE": AN APPROACH

WE DO WELL to recognize our ignorance of China. That ignorance has been perpetuated by two decades of virtual absence of either diplomatic or journalistic contact between the United States and China—a situation which, in the not too distant future, will surely be regarded as a historical oddity of the mid-twentieth century. Moreover, even those Westerners and other non-Chinese who have been permitted extensive residence on the mainland have rarely had an opportunity to observe closely the actual states of mind of individual Chinese. Nor has the regime been interested in revealing much more than its own ideal image of what that state of mind should be.

It is nonetheless possible that we have become too accustomed to a stance of ignorance. For a good deal of significant information has been reaching us—from people coming out of China, from the official press and radio, and from a great variety of semi-official and unofficial writings and speeches (including the celebrated "great-character posters" of the Cultural Revolution)—as recorded by an international coterie of China-watchers, many of them very well informed, whose numbers ever increase. Could it be, then, that our ignorance has to do not so much with "facts" alone as with an inability to make sense of the vast amount of information we do possess? What I am suggesting is that a good part of our ignorance is conceptual.

Indeed, how is one to make sense of the extraordinary events that occurred in 1966 and 1967 as part of the Great Proletarian Cultural Revolution? How is one to understand the dramatic emergence of militant new groups such as the Red Guards and the Revolutionary Rebels who at times seemed all powerful as they pursued their campaigns of "purification" and vilification? The unprecedented and undiplomatic verbal and physical abuse accorded British, French, Russian, Indian, Burmese, and other foreign diplomats? And the still more startling attacks upon Party leaders, along with general undermining of Party authority, including periods of violence and confusion of such magnitude as to suggest complete national chaos and even civil war?

The explanation usually put forth is that there has been a "power struggle," or, allowing for a few complexities, "essentially a power struggle." The implication is that this designation, accompanied by a few comments about political rivalries, explains all. During a visit to Hong Kong in February 1967 I found many Western and Chinese observers, rivaling in agitation the participants in the Cultural Revolution itself, putting forth endless—and endlessly elaborate—speculations on how Liu Shao-ch'i or Lin Piao or Chou En-lai really felt about Mao Tse-tung, or, when these were exhausted, how their wives really felt about one another. Such speculations, when offered as a *total* explanation for the Cultural Revolution, were consistent with certain cultural tendencies affecting the observers: the Chinese inclination to see the world as no more

than a network of human relationships and rivalries; and
the American preoccupation with what might be called
"practical mechanisms" rather than ideological or theoretical considerations.* Without denying the psychological
importance of personal rivalries, the great shortcoming of
the individual-power-struggle theories was their failure to
place such struggles and rivalries within a larger psychological and historical framework. They thus contained a
number of implicit but unexplained and highly dubious
assumptions about "power" and "rivalry" as ultimate human motivations.

A related kind of explanation focused upon the state of
Mao's physical and mental health as the key to everything
taking place. And in Hong Kong in particular one encountered articulate, even passionate, defenders of the point of
view that Mao was in excellent health, severely ill, senile,
mad, or dead. Here too we may say that Mao's physical
and mental health is an important question, but that its
use as *the* explanation of the Cultural Revolution is an
effort to take refuge from complexity by means of an individual "diagnosis." During those early weeks of 1967 all
news from the mainland was seized upon by Hong Kong
China-watchers, but the adherents of the "power-struggle"
and "individual-diagnostic" theories (both often held by
the same people) seemed to be expecting—or at least hop-
ing for—that specific news item that would, once and for
all, supply the missing piece to the puzzle and lay bare the
power struggle or establish the diagnosis.

* The American stress upon mechanism and the Chinese emphasis
upon human relationships are themselves ideological; both can be
thought of as anti-ideological ideologies.

But there have also been, in Hong Kong and elsewhere throughout the world, much more thoughtful approaches to an understanding of the Cultural Revolution. These have stressed such factors as China's (and especially Mao's) "Yenan Syndrome" or "Complex," the nostalgia for the heroic revolutionary methods and achievements of days gone by; China's abrupt loss of a comfortable relationship to her own cultural past; her sense of mounting threat from the outside, especially from America's intervention in Vietnam; and her undergoing a kind of "Protestant-Catholic dispute" between evangelical reawakening and established bureaucratic compromise.[1] All of these interpretations contain considerable truth, and the first in particular illuminates much of what has been occurring. But we have lacked a general perspective within which to comprehend both psychological motives and historical context—that is, a *psychohistorical* framework.

I propose such a framework, however tentative and precarious, because I believe it can reveal much about motivations behind and relationships between seemingly unfathomable and disjointed events, and at the same time possibly contribute to the general understanding of such upheavals, wherever they may occur. My goal is not to reduce the vast canvas of the Cultural Revolution to a set of individual-psychological observations. Rather, I wish to suggest a theoretical perspective which, while unitary, is also open and broadly inclusive, and which stresses shifting symbols and forms in the interplay of the individual with the collective. The approach, then, as I have elsewhere indicated, is most accurately termed that of *psychoformation.*

I should like to suggest that much of what has been taking place in China recently can be understood as a quest for revolutionary immortality. By revolutionary immortality I mean a shared sense of participating in permanent revolutionary fermentation, and of transcending individual death by "living on" indefinitely within this continuing revolution. Some such vision has been present in all revolutions and was directly expressed in Trotsky's ideological principle of "permanent revolution" (even if other things were also meant by this term); but it has taken on unprecedented intensity in present-day Chinese Communist experience.

Central to this point of view is the concept of symbolic immortality I have described in earlier work: of man's need, in the face of inevitable biological death, to maintain an inner sense of continuity with what has gone on before and what will go on after his own individual existence. From this point of view the sense of immortality is much more than a mere denial of death; it is part of compelling, life-enhancing imagery binding each individual person to significant groups and events removed from him in place and time. It is the individual's inner perception of his involvement in what we call the historical process. The sense of immortality may be expressed biologically, by living on through (or in) one's sons and daughters and their sons and daughters; theologically, in the idea of a life after death or of other forms of spiritual conquest of death; creatively, or through "works" and influences persisting beyond biological death; through identification with nature, and with its infinite extension into time and space; or experientially, through a feeling-state—that of experiential transcendence—so intense that, at least temporarily, it eliminates time and death. While this may at first seem a rather abstract approach to the passions and actions of old revolutionaries and young followers, I believe that only by recognizing such life-and-death components of the revolutionary psyche can we begin to comprehend precisely these passions and actions.[2]

Applying these modes of symbolic immortality to the revolutionary, we may say that he becomes part of a vast "family" reaching back to what he perceives to be the historical beginnings of his revolution and extending infinitely into the future. This socially created "family" tends to replace the biological one as a mode of immortality; moreover, it can itself take on an increasingly biological quality, as, over the generations, revolutionary identifications become blended with national, cultural, and racial ones. The revolutionary denies theology as such, but embraces a secular utopia through images closely related to the spiritual conquest of death and even to an afterlife. His revolutionary "works" are all important, and only to the extent that he can perceive them as enduring can he achieve a measure of acceptance of his own eventual death. The natural world to which he allies himself is one that must be transformed by revolution while continuing to contain all that revolution creates. And his experiential transcendence can approach that of religious mystics, as a glance at some of the younger participants in China's Cultural Revolution confirms.

What all this suggests, then, is that the essence of the "power struggle" taking place in China, as of all such "power struggles," is power over death.

II

THE DEATH
OF THE LEADER

CENTRAL to China's recent crisis, I believe, is a form of anxiety related to both the anticipated death of a great leader and the "death of the revolution" he has so long dominated. This death anxiety is shared by leader and followers alike, but we do best to focus for a time upon the former.

It is impossible to know Mao's exact physical or mental state. But let us assume, on the basis of evidence we have, that the seventy-four-year-old (born on December 26, 1893) man has generally been vigorous, that he has experienced rather severe illness in recent years, and that he has always been a man of strong revolutionary passions. We can go a bit further, however, especially on the basis of a valuable interview with him conducted by Edgar Snow, perhaps the American who over the years has been closest to Mao, in January 1965.[1]

Snow found Mao alert, "wholly relaxed," and impressive in his stamina during their four-hour meeting.* He also

* Snow also states that "One of the chairman's doctors informed me that Mao has no organic troubles and suffers from nothing beyond the normal fatigue of his age"; and points out that an interview of that kind, coming as it did at the end of "strenuous weeks" devoted to the National People's Congress, "might have been more speedily

found him "reflecting on man's rendezvous with death and ready to leave the assessment of his political legacy to future generations." Indeed, Snow's general description of the interview suggests a man anticipating, if not preoccupied with, death. Snow reports Mao to have said that "he was going to see God." * And when Snow responded by reassuring Mao that he seemed to be in good condition that evening, Mao Tse-tung "smiled wryly" and expressed some doubt, again saying that he was "getting ready to see God very soon."

We need not dwell on Mao's rather striking use of the theological idiom, other than attributing it to a combina-

---

terminated by a sick man." But he describes watching Mao, after seeing Snow to his car, "brace his shoulders and slowly retrace his steps, leaning heavily on the arm of an aide." Subsequent observations on his health differ, but they suggest that from 1965 through 1967 he was neither completely well nor totally incapacitated. The infrequency of his public appearances and his even rarer public speeches, together with a certain amount of observed bodily rigidity, have led to speculation that he might be suffering from some kind of arteriosclerotic condition, or possibly a form of paralysis agitans (Parkinson's disease). Such conditions could affect the mental state, both through organic damage and compensatory efforts to deny incapacity, with related changes in symbolic organization of thought. But if dysfunction were present it would probably take the form of exaggeration or even caricature of prior psychological tendencies rather than the sudden appearance of totally new ones.

* Snow presents Mao's statements in close third-person paraphrase, rather than direct quotation, in accordance with an agreement he made with Mao's aides. He was able to check his own recollections with a written record kept by one of the Chinese who had been present.

tion of playfulness and perhaps an unconscious inclination —on the part of a man who early in his life had renounced rural supernatural beliefs in favor of Marxist-scientific ones—to hedge his bets a little. When Snow questioned him on the matter, he denied any belief in a deity but observed rather whimsically that "some people who claimed to be well informed said there was a God. There seemed to be many gods and sometimes the same god [when called forth for self-serving political purposes] could take all sides."

More important from our standpoint are the reminiscences that immediately follow—about family members who had died, about his career as a revolutionary, and about the "chance combination of reasons" that had caused him to become interested in the founding of the Chinese Communist Party. Involved here is an old man's nostalgic need to review his past life in relationship to his forthcoming death. That is, death is seen as a test of the quality of one's overall existence. And in the face of a threat of total extinction one feels the need to give form to that existence—to *formulate* its basic connectedness, its movement or development, and above all its symbolic integrity or cohesion and significance.

Prominent among these reminiscences is Mao's sense of being an *eternal survivor*—his recollections of both his brothers having been killed, of the execution of his first wife during the Revolution, and the death of their son during the Korean War. Mao commented that it was "odd" that he had escaped death, that although he was often prepared for it "death just did not seem to want him." He described several narrow escapes from which he emerged unscathed, including one in which he was "splashed all over with the blood of another soldier."

Mao seems to be telling us that his death is both imminent and long overdue. What he considers remarkable is not that so many family members and revolutionary comrades (the two categories become virtually inseparable) have died around him, but that he has in each case been spared. We recognize the survivor's characteristically guilt-laden need to contrast his own continuing life with others' deaths.*

For Mao is surely the survivor *par excellence,* the hero of a truly epic story of revolutionary survival, that of the Long March of 1934–1935, in which it is believed that more than 80 percent of the original group perished along a six-thousand-mile trek in order that the remainder—and the Revolution itself—might stay alive. To transcend his guilt, the survivor must be able to render significant the death immersions he has experienced—and in Mao's case, done much to bring about. This kind of survivor formulation faces both ways: justification of the past and contribution to the future.

Thus, for a man in Mao's position—of his age and special commitments—the affirmation of a sense of immortality becomes crucial. *The overwhelming threat is not so*

---

* There is a suggestion here also of the survivor's sense of "reinforced invulnerability," of having met death and, by means of a special destiny, conquered it. It is this sense that permits the survivor to enter into the myth of the hero, as we shall see to be the case with Mao. But I have found that such feelings can be fragile, and can readily reverse themselves to expose a heightened sense of vulnerability concealed beneath.[2]

much death itself as the suggestion that his "revolutionary works" will not endure.

We sense the passion behind his apparent calm as he goes on, during the same interview, to describe the "two possibilities" for the future: the first, the "continued development of the Revolution toward Communism"; and the second, "that youth could negate the Revolution and give a poor performance: make peace with imperialism, bring the remnants of the Chiang Kai-shek clique back to the Mainland and take a stand beside the small percentage of counter-revolutionaries still in the country." The first is an image of continuous life; the second of death and extinction, of impaired immortality. What he said next—"Of course he did not hope for counter-revolution. But future events would be decided by future generations . . ."—is unexpectedly stark in its suggestion of negative possibility. He is, in other words, far from certain about the fate of his revolutionary works, about the vindication of his own life.

III

THE DEATH
OF THE REVOLUTION

Mao's ultimate dread—the image of extinction that stalks him—is the death of the revolution. When he speaks of the possible "poor performance" of the young, his overriding concern is that the immortal revolutionary legacy will be squandered. As he pointed out to Snow in that same interview, "those in China now under the age of twenty have never fought a war and never seen an imperialist or known capitalism in power." His fear is not simply that the young are too soft, but that they may be incapable of sharing and perpetuating the world view that created the revolution. For that world view was based upon his and his generation's specific experience, and as he goes on to say about the young, "They knew nothing about the old society at first hand. Parents could tell them, but to hear about history and to read books was not the same thing as living it." That is, in such unknowing hands the sacred thing itself—the Revolution—could be abused, neglected, permitted to die.

Such "historical death" can, for the revolutionary, represent an "end of the world," an ultimate deformation and desymbolization.* It may cause anxiety similar to or even greater than that associated with the idea of individual death. Actually, the two forms of death anxiety become inseparable: if the revolution is to be extinguished, the dying revolutionary can envision nothing but the total extinction of his own self.

Maoists repeatedly call forth certain specific images to suggest the danger of the death of the revolution. These include "American imperialism," "feudalism," "the capitalist road," "bourgeois remnants," and "modern revisionism." American imperialism is the ultimate enemy to which one must be alert, lest it destroy the revolution through power or guile. But the threat it poses is external and therefore largely visible. Feudal or capitalist and bourgeois remnants, on the other hand, are doubly dangerous because, as retained internal poisons whose effects are mainly upon the mind, they tend to be invisible. They thus require constant psychic purging, as provided by the extensive programs of thought reform (or "brainwashing") so long prominent in Chinese Communist practice. But what has recently emerged as the greatest threat of all is modern revisionism. For it is both an external danger, as embodied by a visible friend-turned-enemy, the Soviet Union; and an internal one of an insidious personal nature. It is a form of degeneracy or inner death experienced by those who once knew the true path to revolutionary immortality but, through a combination of moral weakness and shadowy conspiracy, strayed from it. Much more than the other

---

* All of these terms refer to symbolic death, through loss of viable relationship to the forms and symbols which sustain psychic life.

negative images, modern revisionism looms as almost an immediate possibility.*

But why now? Why the current crisis in revolutionary immortality? There is much evidence that the Cultural Revolution represents the culmination of a series of conflicts surrounding totalistic visions and national campaigns, of an increasing inability to fulfill the visions or achieve the transformations of the physical and spiritual environment claimed by the campaigns. The conflicts took on great intensity over the decade including the late 1950s and early 1960s, and found their quintessential expression in what was surely the most remarkable campaign of all prior to the Cultural Revolution, the Great Leap Forward of 1958.

I shall later examine more closely the cast of mind associated with the Great Leap, and the technological and psychological impediments involved. It was a heroic attempt to achieve rapid industrialization and collectivization by making extensive use of the bare hands and pure minds of the Chinese people. Its massive failures resulted in overwhelming death imagery in several ways. It produced widespread confusion and suffering even as the regime was announcing its brilliant achievements. And its extensive falsification of statistics reached down, it was later learned, to virtually every level of Party cadre. This

---

* The kind of energy the Chinese Communists have long mobilized against "feudal remnants"—influences from the old society believed to threaten China's future—now seem to be directed against "modern revisionism." The shift in emphasis has great historical significance, but the quality of urgency and danger is psychologically consistent in the two cases.

falsification represented something more than merely a conscious attempt on the part of the regime to deceive the outside world: it was an expression of a powerful need (dictated by pressures from above but by no means limited to government leaders) to maintain a collective image of revolutionary vitality that became, so to speak, more real than reality itself. Such visions of transformation had become so basic to Chinese Communist (and more specifically Maoist) practice—and in many cases had been so brilliantly realized—that they could not be abandoned without a sense that the fundamental momentum of the revolution, its life force, was ebbing. When the disparity between vision and experience became manifest, we suspect earlier confidence in China's revolutionary immortality must have been severely undermined even among those closest to Mao who had in the past shared most enthusiastically in his vision. *Whether one attributed the Great Leap's failure to insufficient revolutionary zeal (as Mao did) or to an excess of the same (as did Liu Shao-ch'i and other "pragmatists"), all came to feel anxious about the life of the revolution.*

The regime's subsequent (1961–1962) economic backtracking and cultural liberalization, apparently implemented by the pragmatists despite Maoist resistance, also contributed to these conflicts. Measures deemed necessary for national recovery encouraged precisely the kinds of personal freedom and self-interest readily viewed within Chinese Communist ideology as decadent "individualism" and "economism." That is, liberalization posed a severe threat to the totalistic vision of absolute subjugation of self to regime upon which the overall claim to revolutionary immortality had been built. The same pattern had occurred before, following the Hundred Flowers episode of 1956–1957, an even more celebrated program of relaxation strongly influenced by Khrushchev's revelations about Stalin, by the Hungarian uprising, and by economic difficulties in China itself. At that time the Chinese shared in the general shattering of the image of infallibility surrounding the Soviet Union as the center of world communism, and this must also have raised questions about their own mode of revolutionary immortality. The liberalization of 1961–1962, following several years of economic strain and general unrest caused by the failure of the Great Leap, did not produce quite the luxuriant across-the-board condemnation of the regime that took place at the time of the Hundred Flowers. But there was nevertheless a muted historical repetition. More important, precisely the things said by many intellectuals during 1961–1962—the demand for de-emphasis of politics and for stress upon learning for its own sake (including greater use of books and equipment from capitalist countries), and especially the mockery of the regime's claim to infallibility—came to be denounced later as signs of "degeneracy" and "decay." The very fruits of liberalization became, for Mao and certain other Chinese leaders, death-tainted threats to the immortal revolutionary vision.

From 1962 onward, and especially since 1965 (when the preliminaries to the Cultural Revolution took place), the regime has been struggling to reassert the confident relationship to history it had possessed in earlier days. The split among Party leaders has had much to do with the image held of just how one should go about doing this.

During the pre-Cultural Revolution decade Mao encountered increasing opposition because of his long commitment to the kind of heroic but unrealizable vision that
reached its zenith in the Great Leap Forward. From at
least 1955 the "pragmatists" (and one must always look
upon the term as relative) within the Party have sought to
moderate this vision and to pursue programs resembling
the less militant Soviet example. They apparently suc-
ceeded in curbing Mao's influence, at least temporarily,
during the late 1950s and early 1960s. This resistance to
Mao, leading to his resignation under pressure from the
State chairmanship in December 1958 (though he did retain chairmanship of the Party throughout), could take
shape only because of the growing conviction that alternatives to his policies were absolutely necessary for economic and social stability. But Mao was later to refer
scornfully to such pragmatists as "women with bound
feet" and to associate their caution with remnants of the
"dying old regime." To Mao and his supporters both his
partial ouster and the programmatic alternatives of his opponents were expressions of betrayal of the revolutionary
vision, evidences of death and deterioration.*

* Peking wall posters reported Mao to have said, in October 1966:
"I was extremely discontented with that decision, but I could do
nothing about it." And Hsiao,[1] without relying on the accuracy of
the wall posters, concludes that "the existing evidence suggests that
Mao gave up his State Chairmanship *not entirely* by his own choice."
But there are some observers who, stressing the importance of doctrine for the Chinese Communists, accept the official version given
out at the time of the decision (December 10, 1958): namely, that
Mao was being relieved of his duties as State Chairman in order to
"make it possible for him to spare more of his time to do the theoretical work of Marxism-Leninism."

Maoists later called forth the picturesque idiom of Chinese folklore to place these critics in the center of a demonology—referring to them as "demons," "devils," "monsters," "ogres," "ghosts," and "freaks." But demonology always addresses itself to the management of life and death, and includes an implicit theory of what might be called negative immortality: incarnations of evil which never die out, whatever one does to counter their nefarious influences. Groups like the Maoists who so boldly defy human limitation are inevitably plagued in turn by images of supernatural enemies. For demonology also reflects unacceptable subterranean conflicts. The "devils" and "monsters" under attack are largely inner doubts of Maoist accusers concerning their own omnipotence; they are in effect anti-immortals.

What are some of these deadly influences? Much of the rhetoric during the Cultural Revolution and the Socialist Education Movement preceeding it has been a reaction and an answer to ideas expressed during the preceeding year (1961–1962), of liberalization. Under attack at the philosophical level have been theories of "human nature" along with expressions of "humanism" (or even "socialist humanism") making their way to China from Russian and Eastern European intellectual circles. For such concepts deny that class origin is the ultimate moral and psychological determinant of behavior, the first by insisting that certain characteristics are shared by all of mankind, and the second through a principle the Chinese contemptuously term "love for all people," under which even capitalists and landlords become worthy of sympathy.

Ideas like these are dangerous because they could undermine the Maoist vision of revolutionary immortality by encouraging people to revert to alternative intellectual traditions which extol quests for truth and self-realization. Or in the somewhat more pejorative language of the Cultural Revolution, they lead to desires "to get on by politics, be really good at your specialty, and have a good life." These ideas emerge from post-Stalinist thought, from "modern revisionism," and express a rediscovery of the individual. But in Chinese media they are dismissed as a "philosophy of survival." Paradoxically, a humanist principle of "love for all people" becomes associated (in Maoist terminology) with "degeneration" into a "petrifying bourgeoisie," with traits that deserve to be "relegated to the morgue." Humanist principles extolling man's life are now seen as agents of death, as demons that must be exorcised lest their deadly emanations destroy all.

The Chinese have also had to cope with a more concrete form of death anxiety, as stimulated by the war in Vietnam and the fear of war with America. There is good evidence that the repeated characterization of America as a "paper tiger" by no means eliminates in Chinese minds images of annihilation associated with her destructive power. And Mao has in the past regularly instituted large-scale programs of reform and "rectification" when preparing for actual military combat. But I believe that the fear of war with America is in itself less of a fundamental source of the Cultural Revolution than an aggravating factor in the overall death anxiety surrounding it. And the Cultural Revolution itself appears to be more a quest for a collective *sense* of revolutionary power than an actual mobilization of military power to combat an outside enemy.

China's crisis, then, involves a profound general threat to revolutionary immortality intertwined with the anxious concern of an aging, partly infirm leader-hero about his capacity, through his revolutionary contributions, to outlive himself. The explosive disruption of a unified revolutionary vision (granting that conflict underlay such unity even in the past) has enormous significance as both cause and effect. For in the absence of such a vision, each individual self becomes vulnerable to the anxiety of extinction associated both with biological death and with collective forms of desymbolization. No wonder that elements of the historical past—of both Chinese tradition and the modern encounter with the West—take on newly ominous qualities. Ghosts and demons must be slain again and again as fear for the life of the revolution becomes associated with fear of the dead. To remain calm, to act with measure in the face of such a threat, can be perceived as an intolerable form of inactivation and stasis. The psychological stage is reached in which one cannot dispense with one's hatred. One cannot give up one's enemies.

IV

THE QUEST
FOR REBIRTH

THE ACTIVIST response to symbolic death—or to what might be called unmastered death anxiety—is a quest for rebirth. One could in fact view the entire Cultural Revolution as a demand for renewal of communist life. It is, in other words, a call for reassertion of revolutionary immortality.

Without losing sight of antagonisms among individual leaders, we do well to consider the significance of the "cultural" in this unique "revolution." We may speak of culture, in its broadest anthropological sense, as an accumulation of significant symbols, or, as Clifford Geertz has recently written, of "symbolic sources of illumination" which each man requires "to put a construction upon events, to orient himself to 'the ongoing course of experienced things.' " [1] Mao seems to have a similarly inclusive view of human culture, but unlike Western anthropologists he feels compelled to regulate its tone and content, at least within his nation, and to take steps to alter it radically when it seems to be moving in undesirable directions.* A cultural revolution anywhere involves a collec-

---

* The idea that the state and its officials should manage the cultural tone of society—should supervise the songs people sing, the rituals they follow, the principles by which they live—goes far back in

tive shift in the psychic images around which life is organized. In Maoist China, however, it has meant nothing less than *an all-consuming death-and-rebirth experience, an induced catastrophe together with a prescription for reconstituting the world being destroyed.*

The "total mobilization of faith" (in Mark Gayn's phrase) involved in this prescription for rebirth has been peculiarly autistic. For more than a year the Chinese turned in upon themselves, performing actions required by their inner states or those of their leaders, however inappropriate or repugnant these actions may have seemed to a perplexed and fascinated outside world. In this sense the Cultural Revolution moves in the direction of what I propose to call *psychism*—the attempt to achieve control over one's external environment through internal or psychological manipulations, through behavior determined by intra-psychic needs no longer in touch with the actualities of the world one seeks to influence.* I shall have much to say about such psychism as a predominant element in the Cultural Revolution's Maoist call to life.

The agents of this attempted rebirth, the Red Guards, reveal much about its nature. The tenderness of their

---

Chinese tradition. It is an aspect of the holistic view of man in his relationship to state, society, and nature that persists in communist practice.

* "Psychism" is an admittedly awkward coinage, but it seems the best term for the phenomenon I wish to describe. Other related words, such as "autism," "psychologism," and "voluntarism" have specific meanings and would be misleading. The concept is relative, and to say that the Cultural Revolution moves in the direction of psychism is by no means to claim that everything its leaders and followers say or do fits into this category.

years—they have included not only youths in their early twenties or late teens but children of thirteen and fourteen —has been striking to everyone, and then much too quickly attributed to political necessity alone. The assumption here is that, having alienated most of the more mature population by his extreme policies, Mao had no choice but to call upon the young. But I believe that one must look beyond such explanations (whatever their partial truth) to the wider symbolism of the Red Guard movement.

According to most accounts, the Red Guards first began to appear during the early summer of 1966. (One Red Guard poster put up at Tsing-hua University Middle School, later named Red Guard Militant School, was dated June 24, and there are other versions that claim an even earlier appearance at Peking University.) Their exact origin remains obscure. One model referred to by the Chinese press is that of a group of guerrilla units during the heroic early days of the Chinese Revolution which bore the same name and were also often very young. Needless to say, there is no reference to the Red Guards of the Russian Revolution, though these were probably the original inspiration for the concept. What is certain is that the present-day People's Liberation Army has served as an important model for the emergence of the new Red Guard of China's Cultural Revolution.

Only after an official public "confirmation" and blessing from Mao Tse-tung during a gigantic dawn rally on August 18, 1966, did the Red Guard take on national and international significance. Within a few days tens of thousands of youngsters with identifying red armbands were roaming through Peking and, before long, the entire country. Some have viewed the Red Guard movement as a spontaneous phenomenon, a point of view encouraged by the regime itself. Most Western observers take the opposite position and see it as carefully shaped throughout by knowing Maoist sculptors. What appears to have taken place is a combination of purposeful manipulation by Maoists and partly autonomous responses and decisions by leaders of Red Guard units—with all behavior profoundly influenced by the immortalizing vision animating the Cultural Revolution. Permitting a certain amount of spontaneity in this kind of movement would be in keeping with Maoist concepts of the revolutionary creativity of the masses, though such concepts would by no means preclude close control over the extent and direction of that spontaneity.

The Maoists certainly were in general control of the Red Guard movement during its early months, much less so during the factional rivalries and general confusion later on. But from the beginning there was probably a good deal of emotion stimulated that went its own way and could not be entirely managed by anyone—as is generally true of mass movements, especially when participants are very young. It is possible the Red Guard, as some have already claimed, could turn out to be a transitional entity, to be dispensed with as soon as it has outlived its usefulness. Even if this is the case, however, one must consider the meaning of the creation of a "youth force" at this time, and the specific functions it was called upon to serve.

From the beginning the battle cry was the triumph of

youth over age, of "the new" over "the old." Hence the Red Guard's announced early goal of totally destroying the "Four Olds" (old ideas, old culture, old customs, and old habits); and the similar stress upon smashing the "old educational system" in its entirety. The formation of the Red Guard was in fact closely tied in with an attack upon teachers, university officials, and educational policies, beginning at Peking University in May–June 1966. This focus upon education has been part of an effort to bring about a shift in qualities of mind that are to be esteemed and rewarded. More important than newness as such (*past* revolutionary virtues were honored) has been an association with youth and vitality. And the human targets selected by the young militants for mental and physical abuse were, in contrast, referred to as "old fogies of the landlord and bourgeois class," "the revisionist clique of old men [on the Peking Party Committee]," and, a bit later, as "old men in authority" and "old gentlemen who follow the capitalist road." The Red Guards themselves were heralded as young people who had "declared war on the old world." But in their attack upon old age and decay they were, psychologically speaking, declaring war upon death itself.

The special aura of the Red Guard had to do not only with its youth but with its class purity. Its members were presented to the general public as an elite organization of youngsters charged with cleansing the entire nation. One could be admitted to their number, at least during those early days, only if one came from a family of workers, of poor (or "middle") peasants, of revolutionary cadres, or of members of the People's Liberation Army. With the rapid expansion of the Red Guard into a mass movement, these standards were inevitably relaxed, but its purity was nonetheless constantly contrasted with the "Five Black" categories of people selected for attack: landlords, rich peasants, counter-revolutionaries, "bad elements," * and rightists.

From this standpoint the August 18 rally launching the Red Guard becomes a momentous historical occasion. Western viewers of an official film of the event shown in Hong Kong and elsewhere were so impressed with the intensity of mass emotion and primal unity evoked that they have compared it to *The Triumph of the Will*, the Nazis' famous film of Hitler at Nuremberg. One of these observers, Franz Schurmann—noting the extraordinary dawn scene of a million people gathered in the great square singing "The East Is Red," Mao Tse-tung powerful in his presence though walking slowly and stiffly (and thereby encouraging rumors of severe illness), then moving out among the masses on the arm of a teen-age girl—went further and spoke of the formation of a "new community." I would suggest that this new community, in a symbolic sense, is a *community of immortals*—of men, women, and children entering into a new relationship with the eternal revolutionary process. An event of this kind is meant to convey *a blending of the immortal cultural and racial sub-*

---

* A rather loosely used term, which in earlier campaigns has referred to various undesirable local types—including those who have connections with the underworld or with remnants of secret societies (prominent in traditional and pre-Communist China), and those who do not engage in productive work.

stance of the Chinese as a people with the equally immortal Communist revolution.

On other occasions as well the Red Guard could convey an image of young people touched by grace, bestowing their anointed state upon everyone around them. A Chinese-speaking Westerner who moved freely among thousands of Red Guards during a visit to Canton in January 1967 described to me an extraordinary scene of "children of thirteen to eighteen with beautiful faces," enjoying themselves enormously and looking "exhilarated" as they chanted, sang, and exhorted one another with the sayings of Mao Tse-tung, all against a backdrop of innumerable pictures of their great leader. While there were a few older supervisors among them, the general image created was not unlike that of a children's crusade. They were a mass of youngsters unified by a transcendent vision, so infused with a sense of virtue as to be almost beatific—politicized "flower children" of the Cultural Revolution.

But the Red Guards, as everyone knows, have also had another face. Theirs has been the task of inducing the catastrophe, of (in their own words) "breaking and smashing," or initiating widespread agitation and disruption while spreading the message that this was what the country required. They became a strange young band of wandering zealots in search of evil and impurity. And during the first year of their existence virtually nothing and no one in China escaped their verbal or physical abuse—including at moments even Mao Tse-tung, in whose name all of their actions were carried out. Repeatedly identifying themselves as "anti-bureaucratic" and "anti-authority," the

Red Guard became the means by which the Maoists undermined the very Party and state structure they had so painfully labored to create over the entire course of the Chinese Revolution. The Red Guard's symbolic mission was to "kill" virtually everything in order to clear the path for national rebirth, leaving only Mao and his Thought as the stuff of that rebirth.

Hence the wide range and often remarkable targets of Red Guard activism, especially during the summer and fall of 1966: the invasion of homes, mainly (but by no means exclusively) those of people in the "Five Black" categories, with confiscation of furniture and other possessions; the humiliation of inhabitants by verbal and sometimes physical abuse, including the ritual of parading them through the streets in dunce caps; the attacks upon temples and churches and the destruction of religious art objects as well as a certain amount of traditional and contemporary (Western-influenced) art; the cutting of hair and removing of leather shoes of Hong Kong visitors, removal from shop windows of clothes considered to be of "queer and alien fashion" even when Chinese-made, and the destruction of foreign-made objects of all kinds, including dolls and playing cards; the replacement of usual burial ceremonies with simple cremation; and the demand that traffic signals be reversed so that red have the properly positive connotation of "go," that the order in military drill be changed from "eyes right" to "eyes left," and that Peking itself be renamed "The East Is Red."

To be sure, these latter demands probably resulted in nothing more than colorful great-character posters, and much else in the Red Guard crusade turned out to be rather short-lived and even improvisational. Yet the crusade had an overall consistency of spirit that was well expressed in the manifesto of one group of middle-school students:

> We are the Red Guards of Chairman Mao and we effect the convulsion. We tear up and smash up old calendars, precious vases, U.S. and British records, superstitious lacquers and ancient paintings, and we put up the picture of Chairman Mao.

All this is seen as part of the general principle of "breaking down the old and establishing the new." But since only revolutionary Maoism is eligible to be designated as "new," everything else—especially that which feels un-Chinese, non-revolutionary, or simply non-Maoist—must be destroyed as "old." The Red Guard was to embody and to demonstrate to all a principle of renewal and an image of perpetual youth—really perpetual life—that was both revolutionary and Chinese.

Whether or not accompanied by physical abuse, the verbal violence of the crusade was impressive. The literature associated with the Red Guards has abounded in gory death imagery. It has sometimes taken the form of a kind of military bravado:

> Demolition bombs and hand grenades will be thrown. . . . Let what is called "human affection" . . . get out of the way!

And at other times it has called forth various biological and anatomical metaphors:

> . . . non-revolutionaries are bad eggs; counter-revolutionaries are broken eggs! . . . They must dig out their guts, change their bones.

Peasant earthiness merges with extreme expressions of class antagonism:

> Old and young gentlemen [of landlord and bourgeois classes], we tell you frankly, you all stink and you are nothing special, just rotten trash. . . . We detest you from our hearts! We hate you! . . . We shall beat [members of these exploiting classes], crunch them. . . . We shall smite their dog mouths and our bayonets shall taste blood!"

There must be no leniency, no reconciliation:

> We want to settle accounts for every drop of this ocean of blood-stained hatred. Nothing will ever be forgotten!

And those victimized are accused of being "vampires" and made to ring "death bells." In this way *alleged evil is linked with death*. The "enemy" is defined as "whoever denies or is opposed to the proletarian [Maoist] line of our Party," followed by the simple statement: *"He will die and we will live!"* Beyond the simple threat, we encounter in this last expression a fundamental psychological impetus for victimization (or what is more gently called "prejudice"): the need to reassert one's own immortality, or that of one's group, by contrasting it with its absolute absence in one's death-tainted victim.*

---

* The language used is sometimes reminiscent of the Old Testament and sometimes of nineteenth-century Chinese anti-missionary and anti-Christian outbursts (though of course often more excessive than either). For this kind of extreme language—demonic, scatological, violent, hysterical—is likely to be called forth in struggles between contending modes of immortality. The process is further intensified by youthful zeal and peasant superstitiousness.[2]

Told and retold during the same period have been stories of heroism, of martyrs who gave their lives to combat military, industrial, cultural, or even natural enemies. The individual Red Guard was to model himself upon them and become the most recent and by far the most ambitious version of the "new man in the socialist era." * His privileged status was in the service of the most privileged of missions: "We are graduating students, the generation that counts in the Chinese and the world revolution." He was in fact to epitomize the unlimited capacity of the community of immortals. One young man expressed this to me vividly when talking about his former Red Guard comrades: "They thought themselves the greatest people in the world. They felt they could do anything."

* This "new man" is also expected to embody what Meisner calls "the original bourgeois virtues"—diligence, frugality, self-discipline, honesty, belief in the moral value of work, and unselfishness. Meisner views these as part of an "ascetic pattern of life demanded by Chinese Communist ideology . . . as a means by which men can transform themselves and transform nature to realize the 'truly human life' that in Marxist theory is historically located in the socialist utopia of the future." 3 What I am suggesting is that this ascetic ideal, much like the Calvinist equivalent Meisner also mentions, is bound up with a transcendent involvement. While the Calvinists sought to "establish the Kingdom of God on earth," the Maoists seek a Kingdom of eternal revolution.

V

PURITY

AND POWER

A KEY to the momentum of the Cultural Revolution is the merging of purity and power. We may define "purity" as encompassing such things as self-denial (or even self-surrender) on behalf of a higher cause, the urge to eliminate evil, and ideological single-mindedness. And we may speak of "power" as either the ability to make decisions and take actions that exert control and influence over others, or as the sense of inner strength and capacity. Too often an either/or situation is assumed to exist in which purity or power must be radically subservient to the other as *the* basic motivation for behavior. In regard to present-day China the consensus of outside observers has been that an image of purity has been no more than a decoy and a mask for the power-hunger lurking beneath. But the assumption can be highly misleading. Rather than constituting antagonistic motivations, purity and power are in fact psychologically inseparable.

Both are ultimately associated with some kind of divine, or at least more than human, image. Purity is "godlike" and "god-given" in the sense of virtue so absolute that it transcends mortal frailty, and of influences or "works" that outlast any individual life. Power is godlike in the more

ominous sense of *hubris,* of man usurping divine preroga-
tives, looking upon himself as a god. But in a less pejorative image power is god-given because it is attributed
either to an immortal legacy—the Mandate of Heaven or
Divine Right of Kings*—or to an individual "gift" for ruling men that is virtually superhuman. Interwoven themes
of power and purity are therefore likely to dominate any
collective quest for transcendence. They readily give rise to
forms of ideological totalism so prominent in the Chinese
Revolution. And the accompanying polarization of good
and evil leads to distinctions between "people" and "non-
people," to decisions concerning which groups are entitled
to exist and which are not, or to what I have called the
dispensing of existence[2]—all in the name of superior virtue. Power becomes the harnessing of purity for an immortal quest.

Mao's previously quoted misgivings about the young as
revolutionary heirs concern their capacity to maintain a
proper combination of purity and power. And his fearful
image of the "death of the revolution" is one of breakdown
of the combination with disintegration of both elements.
The Red Guards were mobilized to confront this break-

* These concepts are by no means the same. The Divine Right of
Kings suggests authority originating with God through the ruler's
distant ancestors, and responsibility only to God. The Mandate of
Heaven suggests a much more contingent authority—"not a patent
of divine right, irrevocable and eternal . . . [but] conferred upon
a sage King whose virtue had entitled him to act as the deputy of
Heaven. His descendents enjoyed it only so long as their virtue made
them worthy representatives of the Supreme Ancestor." [1] What the
two concepts share is a stress upon a transcendent (or immortal)
source of authority.

down by simultaneously "seizing power" for the Maoists and transforming ubiquitous contamination into all-consuming purity.

Two features of the Cultural Revolution epitomize this purity-power constellation: the temporary use of the Paris Commune of 1871 as a model; and, much more important, the dual role of the Army.

The idea of the Paris Commune was consistent with the regime's longstanding communal ethos, and was a means of extending that ethic from the countryside to the city. Images surrounding the Paris Commune, although apparently used ambivalently and experimentally, may have nonetheless influenced the general course of the Cultural Revolution.[3] For the Paris Commune has always had a special mystique for communist movements throughout the world. Its early occurrence and heroic circumstances, and the later commentaries on it by Marx, Engels, and Lenin, have given it a quasi-sacred aura within the sequence of Marxist history. These commentaries dealt with both sides of the constellation we have been discussing: the achievement of proletarian purity by means of collective revolutionary action, and the question of "seizure of power." Like the Cultural Revolution, the Paris Commune stressed the theme of the "armed populace"—the idea of militant unprofessionals—to carry out the two aspects of the mission.

It was Marx himself who pointed out the immortalizing nature of the Paris Commune when he said that it "admitted all foreigners to the honor of dying for an immortal cause." These days it would be difficult to read such a passage without a sense of irony—except perhaps in China.

And the Chinese did indeed use similar language in reference to the Shanghai Commune in February 1967, when they spoke of "the birth of a new Paris Commune in the sixties of this century . . . [through which] the people of Shanghai have been liberated a second time," and which would be "eternal and indestructible." * Their estimate turned out to be a bit premature, since the life of the Shanghai Commune, like that of many institutional arrangements during the Cultural Revolution, turned out to be a very short one. But the point here is the Shanghai Commune's ideal (like that of its model) of perfect fusion of power and purity—through absolute proletarianization, total elimination of bureaucratic and bourgeois "contamination," and close attention to the task of prevailing militarily and politically over one's opponents.

The People's Liberation Army provides an even more striking contemporary purity-power model. The Army's own cultural revolution preceeded that of the rest of the country, and set the tone and idiom for the national movement—with emphasis upon the almost legendary achievements of the Red Army in the past. Thus, Red Guards could refer to a journey to Peking from a distant part of

* There was even a parallel during the Cultural Revolution to Marx's statement about "foreigners." Mao's essay "In Memory of Norman Bethune," originally written in 1939, was given great stress as one of the "three constantly read articles," and in it Mao speaks of this Canadian physician who served with the Chinese Communist Army as having "died a martyr at his post." Mao then asks, "What kind of spirit is this that makes a foreigner selflessly adopt the cause of the Chinese people's liberation as his own? It is the spirit of internationalism, the spirit of communism, from which every Chinese Communist must learn." [4]

China as a "long march." Maoist functionaries became so infused with this military idiom that they extended it to social and economic areas and would (as one Western commentator put it) "treat . . . capital formation as a type of guerrilla warfare." [5] And when leading Peking Opera repertory groups came under attack by Mao himself as "still under the rule of the dead," their road of reform was incorporation into "the great school for the great thought of Mao Tse-tung—the Chinese People's Liberation Army." Through this blend of art and Army, Mao's wife, the former film actress Chiang Ch'ing, emerged from relative obscurity to take a surprisingly active part in the Cultural Revolution. From the outset the ultimate ethic held out to the nation was that of the brave soldier inspired to superhuman sacrifices by the Thought of Mao Tse-tung, then dying willingly and heroically for the revolution with Mao's words on his lips. And groups associated with the Army (as the same observer commented) "offer [ed] instruction to virtually the entire population in communist morality and ethics." *

There is no ignoring the obvious political benefit—indeed, as things turned out, necessity—of backing up the desired psychic state with military strength. Nor did the Army itself, or for that matter its Red Guard emulators, turn out to be totally "pure." Both remained under the general control of the Maoist group, but experienced a va-

* There was something of a historical precedent for this, as the famed Eighth Route Army is said to have served a similar function in Yenan and the Border Areas from about 1938 to 1945. But that was in the midst of civil war, when virtually everybody had to be part of the Army, in contrast to the much more differentiated society in which the Army "offers instruction" today.

riety of factional struggles and conflicts involving Maoists, anti-Maoists, and indeterminate units and subdivisions. Moreover, the Army's entry into the "Triple Alliance" * could be said to represent a certain amount of backtracking from the purist model of the Paris Commune, which the Alliance actually replaced. The same may be said of the increasing hegemony of the Army within the Alliance itself, to the extent of sometimes rendering it virtually a form of military rule. Yet while the resistance Mao encountered made it necessary for him to resort increasingly to military force, that force, from the beginning of the Cultural Revolution, had been intimately associated with revolutionary purity—with combined psychic and material power.

Precisely this combination has been prominent all through Chinese Communist practice. An excellent example is the thought reform process, long a trademark of Chinese communism, with its group-mediated psychological pressures toward ideological conversion. One could view the process as a carrot-and-stick application of power for the purpose of controlling behavior—using various kinds of coercion and threat, together with a promise that those properly reformed will merge with and partake deeply of the invincible revolutionary force. But one could also view it as a method of individual purification which, by means of detailed self-examination, provides benefits akin to those of psychotherapy and spiritual enlighten-

---

* The Triple Alliance includes revolutionary mass organizations such as the Red Guard and Revolutionary Rebels, pro-Maoist cadres (from among officials, Party members, and Party workers), and the People's Liberation Army.

ment. Thought reform has, at various times and for different individuals, been both. All of its elements have been
perpetuated with new intensity during the Cultural Revolution: the familiar insistence that "the [ideologically]
sick be cured," that they "lighten their burdens" and "obtain merits to redeem their crimes"; and the endless public
accusations, self-criticisms, and confessions.

We shall soon note the psychological pitfalls of the
thought reform program as applied during the Cultural
Revolution, but there is no denying the potential impact of
its particular ingredients. Its attractive purity backed by
coercive power—one could equally say attractive power
backed by coercive purity—undoubtedly evoked strong
feelings of self-condemnation, encompassing both guilt
and shame, in many of those failing to meet the extreme
standards of the environment. Such feelings can culminate
in a terrifying anxiety of extinction, related less to biological death per se than to a sense of being cut off from all
human connection and rendered totally inert and insignifi-
cant.

Purity and power merge in the language of the two leaders of the Cultural Revolution, Mao Tse-tung and Lin
Piao, the latter through quotation and paraphrase often
serving as the voice of the former. Lin Piao thus states,
"All our work is preparation for war"; and also, "The best
weapon of our troops is not the airplane, cannon, tank,
or atomic bomb, but the thought of Mao Tse-tung; the
greatest fighting force is man armed with the thought
of Mao Tse-tung, daring, not afraid of death." Lin and

others frequently quoted statements by Mao to the effect that "War can be abolished only by war, and in order to get rid of the gun it is necessary to take up the gun"; and "The world can be changed only by using gun barrels" (a recent modification of Mao's earlier principle that "political power grows out of the barrel of a gun"). What this language suggests is *the principle that ultimate purity requires application of ultimate power, but that purity as such remains the source of that power—indeed is ultimate power—because he who possesses it has conquered death.*

The Mao-Lin combination can itself be said to symbolize just this kind of fusion. While Mao may be considered to embody both purity and power, he has (or had prior to the Cultural Revolution) achieved a status within revolutionary lore as godlike in wisdom and virtue. Lin, although associated with revolutionary education and reform, is the essence of the successful military man, his aura of power deriving not only from longstanding Army leadership but from close recent identification with the making and testing of nuclear weapons. And during the Cultural Revolution both men have stood not only for the much publicized motto "Seize power!" but for the related one, "Seize the Revolution!"—the latter much more significant because of its implicit suggestion of noble purpose and enduring consequence.

The "mass line" and the almost identical "Red line" are ideological manifestations of a similar blend. They have been employed, at times loosely and at times with the most narrow precision, to provide criteria for acceptable behavior during the Cultural Revolution, just as they did during earlier campaigns and in everyday life in Communist China. But in terms of feeling, they evoke a more mystical sense of immortal revolutionary substance, and serve as a guide for an individual's becoming and remaining part of that substance. Moreover, the Cultural Revolution has stressed a mobilization of purity through China's power of numbers—visions of seven hundred million Chinese all following the "mass line" and achieving "the peasant and worker viewpoint"—which is another way of combining revolutionary substance with the eternal substance of the Chinese race and culture.

A related issue is the heightening during the Cultural Revolution of the longstanding Chinese Communist preoccupation with being "Red" as distinct from "expert." This seemingly simple polarity reflects a crucial confrontation between revolutionary purity and modern technology. Without pausing just yet to explore this confrontation, we may say that the extreme Maoist glorification of "Redness" and undermining of "expertness" (the latter including not only professional skill but learning itself) for a time so threatened the last vestiges in China of dispassionate intellectual endeavor as to virtually eliminate "the intellectuals" as a functioning group. (The extreme example was the public humiliation of Kuo Mo-jo, President of the Chinese Academy of Sciences, long the epitome of the Communist intellectual and perhaps the most nationally respected of all Chinese scholars.) Involved here is the implicit assumption that the special revolutionary combination of purity and power could in itself completely nourish the individual mind, and that any additional intellectual needs were suspect.

In the delineation of purity great stress was placed upon

what could be considered rural and "Chinese" as opposed to the threatening *im*purities of the urban and the foreign. While the Red Guards first appeared in Peking, they came to include many youths from outside the large cities and in general tried to take on a rural coloring. They made repeated journeys to the countryside and placed great stress upon "learning from the peasants" and "becoming little students of the masses"—these two slogans having been prominent in the preceding Socialist Education Movement, which sent large numbers of intellectuals to rural areas to imbibe the wisdom of the Chinese earth and its tillers. Here we sense a restorationist impulse, the Maoist attempt to recapture a form of harmony (purity) felt to exist in the past among people close to the earth until "contaminated" by the complexities of modern existence.*

What of the shift in target, within a month or two after the Red Guards came into being, from "class enemies" to "those in authority"? Once it became clear that none other than the head of state, Liu Shiao-ch'i, was to become the object of extreme vituperation, many observers concluded that here was the answer to the mystery of the Cultural Revolution, the entire point of the operation. But even if

---

* This form of harmony and purity is consistent with the "spirit of Yenan" not to mention that of Rousseau. But it is also consistent with various millenary visions of traditional and modern Chinese thinkers, who, in characteristic restorationist fashion, find their models in a mythical golden age of the past. The larger or "Great Harmony" sought in these visions should be distinguished from the more humble everyday Chinese cultural principle of harmonious human relationships, based upon proper attention to rites, principles, and compromise—though the two would seem to have considerable psychological relationship.

one assumes that Mao and Lin had planned from the outset to undermine Liu's authority, and that this goal greatly
influenced the tone and scope of the Cultural Revolution,
one must still ask why it became so important to get rid of
Liu. What was there about this "rivalry for power" that
could cause a revolutionary movement with an extraordinary forty-five-year record of organizational accomplishment prior and subsequent to its assumption of national
power, to embark upon a series of actions directly undermining the authority it had so laboriously built up?

It seems clear that Liu, during the decade prior to the
Cultural Revolution, emerged as a leading voice among
the pragmatists who opposed Mao and sought to limit his
power. There is also some evidence that a group of high
Party officials might have contemplated a *coup d'état*
(even if this is true, however, one does not know whether
Liu was in any way connected with it). But again I would
insist that we avoid the solipsistic assumption that in such
situations men act only out of motives totally centered
upon the individual self, that is, out of "petty jealousies."
Rather, one must assume that Liu came to feel that curbing Mao's power was necessary for the Revolution, just as
we know Mao and his followers to have come to believe
that revitalizing the Revolution required that Liu and his
influence be destroyed.

*In other words the individual urge to wield power is as-
sociated with a formulation which connects that power to
worthy purposes extending beyond both the self and the
historical moment.* Nor can such a formulation be dismissed as mere rationalization of personal ambition. For
ambition itself is bound up with a larger vision, a *control-*

ling image, of self and world: for Liu an image of "de-Maoization" and a pragmatic course of consolidation; for Mao one of heroic national struggle including a spirit that the Chinese themselves call "revolutionary romanticism." Whatever the extent of personal antagonism between the two men, their "power struggle" is enmeshed in questions of purity. Maoist anxiety arises less from the prospect of the Revolution falling into the hands of a different leader, which must in any case inevitably happen, than from the possibility that the new leader will espouse an alternative —and therefore impure—revolutionary vision.

In such instances judgments become retroactive. Four and a half decades of shared revolutionary experience extending from heroic early days through turbulent recent accomplishments, as well as regional bonds so important in Chinese culture (both men are from Hunan province) —all this must give way to a new Maoist claim that Liu had *always* possessed hidden inclinations toward capitalism. The same applies to Liu's celebrated pamphlet "How To Be a Good Communist." Long a source book for the self-cultivation of generations of Party cadres, its forceful combination of Confucianist and Leninist tones always regarded as highly "Maoist," it now becomes the work of a "traitor" which has "poisoned" the minds of innumerable innocent comrades.

Do Mao and his followers really believe this? Or do they coolly regard their own denunciations as no more than necessary political maneuvers? From what I have learned about the behavior of men in such situations (including observations of former Chinese Communist cadres) and about the psychology of belief in general, I would suspect that both tendencies coexist. A sense of tactical necessity merges with the accuser's partial commitment to his own accusations. But the inner logic is tortuous (though perhaps less so for the very young who have not known Liu during his greatest days). And the kinds of judgments made are precisely those which can be equally rapidly reversed once Mao's hegemony has ended (as in the post-Stalinist Russian experience, in which previously condemned leaders, living and dead, had their names cleared and their virtue restored). Yet the original condemnation is felt to be necessary because, in the psychological language we have been using, once a man and his vision are perceived as destroyers of revolutionary immortality, so must be all of his "works." *

Crucial to the blending of power and purity—because it

---

* Confirming the importance of elements beyond the self in the struggle between Communist leaders is the fact that the attack upon Liu has had a highly symbolic quality. Rather than seeking to punish or eliminate Liu—that is, either put him to death or imprison him— Maoists have preferred to condemn him as a dangerous *example* of the kind of deadly impurity that could affect anyone. Throughout the attack upon him he was referred to as "the top party person taking the capitalist road" or "China's Khrushchev." Not until March 1968, months after the collective passions of the Cultural Revolution had subsided, was his actual name reportedly mentioned—and even then not on a public occasion but at a meeting with a Japanese trade delegation presided over by Chou En-lai. This specific identification led some observers to believe that the Maoists were ready to go ahead with a political purge (Liu has remained technically the regime's President throughout, though divested of state functions and confined to his home) and possibly with some form of punitive action. There is some precedent in Chinese tradition for this form of symbolic attack; it was, for instance, utilized by Boxer leaders in 1900 in their public humiliation of members of Allied legations.

draws directly upon both—is the question of autonomy. Even if "the masses," when called upon to "organize their own strength," were actually being manipulated from above, many could nonetheless experience a feeling of awakened individual significance. I have mentioned the sense of unlimited capacity or power in many Red Guards during the more enthusiastic moments of the Cultural Revolution. Along with Revolutionary Rebels and related groups, they roamed the cities and countryside in 1966 and 1967, attacking alleged class enemies, spreading terror among foreign diplomatic communities, and then turning their wrath upon their own "men in authority who take the capitalist road," right on up to the head of state; we suspect that they experienced a rare sense not only of participating in a great moral crusade but of taking matters *into their own hands.*

They could also share in a sense of dramatic reversal of past intimidation and humiliation, at the hands of foreign powers (represented, actually or symbolically, by the diplomats who were abused), of landlords and capitalists (the "class enemies" and "Five Black" categories), and of Communist Party bureaucrats ("those in authority who take the capitalist road"). The attack upon bureaucracy in particular called forth powerful emotional responses in a society which for two thousand years, whatever the regime in power, has subjected its people to the arrogances, dogmatic rigidities, and humiliating controls of a uniquely influential bureaucratic elite. This kind of abuse, along with the struggles of the common people to alleviate it, has been prominently depicted in Chinese fiction, notably in the great and extremely widely read (especially among

the present generation of Chinese Communist leaders)
fourteenth-century historical novel which has been translated into English as *Romance of the Three Kingdoms.* *

In one sense, then, the Cultural Revolution was an ex-
hilarating revolt of the patronized. It was a violent renun-
ciation of what I have elsewhere called "counterfeit nurturance"—situations in which the weak must remain dependent upon the strong for help they both require and
deeply resent as a reminder of their weakness. It has been
an upsurge of the downtrodden. Peasants, impoverished
workers, and even children could convey wisdom to intellectuals, depose government authorities, and win (or so
they were told) the great struggles "between man and
man" and "between man and nature." They could at least
momentarily eliminate painful vestiges of enforced dependency and helplessness.

The paradox is that collective autonomy of this kind results from the totalistic attack upon any signs of the independent (non-Maoist) self. Any violation of the individual
becomes acceptable if in the service of the larger vision.
As a Red Guard was once quoted as saying, "So long as it
is revolutionary, no action is a crime." The goal of each person, the Chinese press made clear, was to become a "stain-

* The other side of the Chinese bureaucratic impulse has been the
extraordinary organizational accomplishments it has brought about:
the governing of so vast and populous a society according to consistent ethical and legal standards. But such a bureaucratic emphasis
is bound to give rise to potentially explosive antagonisms. The Communist bureaucracy has apparently been prone to abuses and forms
of self-indulgence comparable to those of its traditional predecessors;
and some of the Maoist condemnation of it is reminiscent of Milovan
Djilas' attack upon the privileged Communist "New Class."

less screw" in the "locomotive of revolution." * Each was, moreover, warned to beware of the danger of unauthentic claimants to noble ideals—to "tear off the 'Liberty, Equality, Fraternity' loincloth of the bourgeois class." For should class enemies be permitted any liberties, they become "smiling tigers," and one must remember that "smiling tigers can eat people."

The great dread is that the Revolution will be devoured in this fashion, that China will "change color" and take the capitalist-revisionist road. But since it is an ultimate confrontation between good and evil—"a life-and-death struggle on which the fate of the world depends"—a sense of ultimate purity and ultimate power beckon to the individual participant. Even if he cut himself off from all but the most ritualistic Maoist images, he could feel a new autonomy as he merged with his people, his history, his revolution.

---

* The Maoist demand for "absolute selflessness"—and denunciation of "the concept of self-interest, selfishness, advancing one's own interest at the expense of others; and extreme individualism" as "the kernel of the bourgeois world outlook"—finds some cultural echoes in the traditional Chinese stress upon subjugating the individual to prevailing collective standards.[6] But in its more extreme expressions (as during the Cultural Revolution) Maoism leaves considerably less room for certain forms of individual maneuver traditionally permitted under the concept of consideration for "human feelings."

VI

THE IMMORTALIZATION
OF WORDS

How ARE we to understand that remarkable entity, the Thought of Mao Tse-tung? The man and his words fused into a powerful image, which became the essence of revolutionary immortality as well as the energizer for its quest.

This is by no means the first time that a political leader has been made into a divinity. But few in the past could have matched Mao in the superlatives used, the number of celebrants, or the thoroughness with which the message of glory has been disseminated. Even more unique has been the way in which the leader's words have become vehicles for elevating him, during his lifetime, to a place above that of the state itself or its institutional source of purity and power, in this case the Party.* And the process is rendered

---

* This is in violation of the Stalinist precedent of viewing the leader as subservient to and an instrument of the ultimate historical authority of the Party. One would have to go back to Lenin or possibly Marx to find communist analogies to this aspect of the Maoist image; and their deification differed both in being a retrospective historical phenomenon that had to await their deaths, and in being less directly related to specific quotations from their writings. But if one compares Mao to a traditional Chinese emperor (as has Yuji Muramatsu in "Revolution and Chinese Tradition in Yenan Communism" [1]), his position becomes that of a Confucian ruler whose

all the more impressive by the opposite tendency predominant throughout the world—the desacralization of men, words, and virtually everything else. Rather than resort to the tone of uneasy contempt so frequent in Western observers, we do better to take a closer look at some of the psychological and historical currents involved.

All cultures have a way of rendering sacred the word ("In the beginning was the Word, and the Word was with God, and the Word was God"); and none more than China. Relevant here is the Confucian focus upon the *name* as a means of ordering all human life. The traditional principle of "rectification of names" required not only that each live according to the rules governing his category of existence ("Let the ruler be ruler, the minister be minister; let the father be father and the son, son"), but that where disparity existed, the *man* undergo whatever moral change was required for him to fit the name. As Granet has written: "The name possesses the individual rather than the individual possess[ing] the name. It is inalienable." [2]* We may say that the "name"—for example, family name—was the immortal element toward which lay the major responsibility of the individual, himself a mere transient. Only through harmony with the name could a man achieve true "sincerity" or "the way of Heaven"—a place within the immortal rhythms that provided a Chinese equivalent to a state of grace.

The nature of Chinese characters, and traditional atti-

Mandate of Heaven places him above the machinery of state in carrying out what he deems to be best for the masses.

*Granet referred here to the family, but the principle applies to Chinese society in general.

tudes toward them, also enhance the power of the word. As ideographs, or what might be called formative images, they possess an evocative symbolic force (what Arthur Wright calls "weight"[3]) beyond that of words in alphabetical scripts.* Moreover, the traditional education and examination systems were so arranged that the memorization of specific groups of characters—those containing the society's ideal moral image of itself—was one's access to public life. This in turn meant entering what was for the Chinese a special realm of recorded history, so that one's relationship to words became a major path to symbolic immortality.

Within its own idiom Chinese Communism has perpetuated much of this kind of emphasis, and it is in such a cultural context that one must view Mao's own way with words. He has by no means been merely the bearer of venerable tendencies. Rather he has made use over the years of a word-centered tradition in the special fashion of a great contemporary leader.

Western students of Mao's thought have had some difficulty explaining the sources of its power. While often disagreeing on the question of whether Mao has demonstrated originality as a Marxist, most have rightly stressed his persistent preoccupation with themes of "struggle" and "contradictions" and "rectification" and reform. But what has not been adequately recognized, I believe, is a characteristic quality of tone and content that, more than any

---

* Paper with writing on it was venerated, and gathering together discarded scraps of such paper was a deed worthy of having recorded in one's official biography. These attitudes and practices, moreover, continued into the early part of the twentieth century.

other, shaped the psychic contours of the Cultural Revolution. I refer to a kind of *existential absolute, an insistence upon all-or-none confrontation with death.* Mao always further insists that the confrontation be rendered meaningful, that it be associated with a mode of transcendence. One must risk all, not only because one has little to lose but because even in death one has much to gain.

This quality of thought is amply illustrated by many selections contained in the little red bible of the Cultural Revolution, *Quotations from Chairman Mao Tse-tung.*[4] One important chapter takes its title from Mao's 1944* essay "Serve the People," which was one of the most emphasized of all of his writings over the course of the entire movement. The chapter begins with a quotation advocating that all "serve the Chinese people heart and soul" and ends with two comments about death and dying taken from the 1944 essay. The first presents a simple definition of a "worthy death":

> Wherever there is struggle there is sacrifice, and death is a common occurrence. But we have the interests of the people and the sufferings of the great majority at heart, and when we die for the people it is a worthy death.

The cautionary sentence that follows—"Nevertheless, we should do our best to avoid unnecessary sacrifices"—does not alter the message. The second and more probing passage makes use of a classical image:

---

* Recent scholarship has revealed alterations by Maoist compilers in the dating and content of some of these essays; but I generally follow the official versions put forth during the Cultural Revolution as most relevant to my purposes.

All men must die, but death can vary in its significance. The ancient Chinese writer Szuma Chien said, "Though death befalls all men alike, it may be heavier than Mount Tai or lighter than a feather." To die for the people is heavier than Mount Tai, but to work for the fascists and die for the exploiters and oppressors is lighter than a feather.

Here "weight" is equated with lasting significance: * a death becomes "heavier than Mount Tai" because it contributes to the immortal revolutionary process of the Chinese people. Mao encourages everyone to cultivate such a death and thereby, during life, enhance his individual *sense* of immortality.

Another chapter, "War and Peace," contains passages (from essays originally written during the late thirties) that condemn unjust war but extol revolutionary war as "an antitoxin which not only eliminates the enemy's poison but also purges us of our own filth," and as "endowed with tremendous power [which] can transform many things or clear the way for their transformation." There is Mao's proud declaration: "Yes, we are advocates of the omnipotence of revolutionary war; that is good, not bad, it is Marxist." Here "omnipotence" refers on one level to policy priority, but on another to a sense of unlimited revolutionary power called forth by the purifying experience of facing death on behalf of a just cause.

This sentiment is repeated in another chapter, which stresses what is probably the most famous of all Maoist

* This second meaning, namely "important," is also conveyed by the original Chinese term *"chung,"* translated as "weight"; similarly, the Chinese term for "light," *"ch'ing,"* also means "unimportant."

images as revealed in its title, "Imperialism and All Reactionaries Are Paper Tigers." An extract from a speech made in Moscow in 1957 is notable:

> I have said that all the reputedly powerful reactionaries are merely paper tigers. The reason is that they are divorced from the people. Look! Was not Hitler a paper tiger? Was Hitler not overthrown? I also said that the Tsar of Russia, the Empress of China, and Japanese imperialism were all paper tigers. As we know, they were all overthrown. U.S. imperialism has not yet been overthrown and it has the atom bomb. I believe it also will be overthrown. It, too, is a paper tiger.

We can begin to see that the "paper tiger" image is meant to suggest a fundamental hollowness and weakness associated with the absence of immortal revolutionary substance. Therefore, the psychic logic goes, these hollow enemies ("divorced from the people") should pose no threat to the Maoist possessor of that immortal substance.

Above all, one need not fear death at the hands of the enemy—as suggested in a passage published originally in 1938 in an important military volume, *Basic Tactics:*

> When we see the enemy, we must not be frightened to death like a rat who sees a cat, simply because he has a weapon in his hands. We must not be afraid of approaching him or infiltrating into his midst in order to carry out sabotage. We are men, the enemy is also composed of men, we are all men so what should we fear? The fact that he has weapons? We can find the way to seize his weapons. All we are afraid of is getting killed by the enemy. But when we undergo the oppression of the enemy to such a point as this, how can anyone still fear death? And

if we do not fear death, then what is there to fear about the enemy? So when we see the enemy, whether he is many or few, we must act as though he is bread that can satisfy our hunger, and immediately follow him.

Underneath the assumption of oppression being worse than death is a characteristically Maoist *tone of transcendence,* a message to the revolutionary which seems to say that death does not really exist for him; he has absolutely nothing to fear. Mao put forth this message as early as 1919 in the midst of the stirrings of cultural and political revolution associated with the epochal May Fourth Movement:

> What is the greatest force? The greatest force is that of the union of the popular masses. What should we fear? We should not fear heaven. We should not fear ghosts. We should not fear the dead. We should not fear the bureaucrats. We should not fear the militarists. We should not fear the capitalists.

To eliminate awe of seemingly powerful enemies, Mao adopts an attitude of general leveling and de-immortalization ("We are men, the enemy is also composed of men, we are all men so what should we fear?"). But this leveling is mere prelude to claiming that immortal status for his own revolutionary group, and declaring its consequent immunity to the emanations from ordinary arbiters of life and death, supernatural and historical. The revolutionary, then (as Mao also wrote in *Basic Tactics*), can wholeheartedly "resolve to fight to the death to kill the enemy."

A leader who can instill these transcendent principles in his followers can turn the most extreme threat and disinte-

gration into an ordered certainty of mission, convert the most incapacitating death anxiety into a death-conquering calm of near-invincibility. He can in fact become the omnipotent guide sought by all totalist movements—precisely the meaning of the characterization of Mao during the Cultural Revolution as the "Great Leader, Great Teacher, Great Supreme Commander, and Great Helmsman." The Thought of Mao becomes not so much an exact blueprint for the future as a "Way," a call to a particular mode of being on behalf of a transcendent purpose.*

Behind this Way are two psychological assumptions long prominent in Mao's thought but never so overtly insisted upon as during the Cultural Revolution. The first is an image of the human mind as infinitely malleable, capable of being reformed, transformed, and rectified without limit. The second is a related vision of the will as all-powerful, even to the extent that (in his own words) "the subjective creates the objective." That is, man's capacity for both undergoing change and changing his

---

* Franz Schurmann somewhat similarly refers to Mao's thought as "practical ideology" rather than "pure ideology." By practical ideology he means a combination of Marxist-Leninist theory (pure ideology) and everyday practice. Schurmann views Mao's thought as highly flexible and changeable according to the immediate problems confronted ("Mao's creation of thought is a continuing process without any foreseeable conclusion").[5] But what I am referring to is less ideology as such than a quality of feeling, a tenor of action, a form of relating to the world. Thus, what I call Mao's existential absolute—and the Way he has charted around it—are not open-ended or subject to change. They may vary in intensity from time to time, but they have been strikingly consistent in Mao's revolutionary style and throughout his adult life in general.

environment is unlimited; once he makes the decision for change, the entire universe can be bent to his will. But again the controlling image is the sense of revolutionary immortality that confers these vaulting capacities upon the mind. And the key to psychic malleability and power —the central purpose of the thought reform process—is the replacement of prior modes of immortality (especially the biological one provided by the Chinese family system) with the newer revolutionary modes: those of the biosocial revolutionary "Family," of enduring revolutionary "works," and of transcendent revolutionary enthusiasm.

A remarkable feature of the Cultural Revolution has been its concretization of this entire process, so that Mao the man and the "Thought of Mao Tse-tung" converge in an *immortalizing corpus*. Mao came to be regularly described in the Chinese press as "the greatest genius today," and all were assured that "Where the thought of Mao Tse-tung shines, there people see the way to fight for their liberation and there is hope for the victory of revolution." Also highly significant was the merging of this man-thought corpus with the larger immortal cultural-revolutionary substance we have spoken of, the merging of Mao with "the masses":

> Chairman Mao . . . has the greatest trust in and the greatest concern for the masses, and the greatest support for their revolutionary movements and initiative. Chairman Mao throws in his lot with the masses and his heart is always at one with the hearts of the masses. We must turn Chairman Mao's trust and concern into fresh fighting strength and win new victories in the Great Proletarian Cultural Revolution.

The Maoist corpus then takes on the important function of serving as "a fundamental watershed" for distinguishing people from non-people:

> Chairman Mao is the great standard bearer of the international communist movement of the contemporary age, the most beloved and revered leader of the Chinese people and revolutionary peoples of the world. The thought of Mao Tse-tung is contemporary Marxism-Leninism of the highest level, a powerful ideological weapon against imperialism, revisionism, and dogmatism. To support or oppose Chairman Mao and the thought of Mao Tse-tung is a fundamental watershed dividing Marxism from revisionism, and revolution from counter-revolutionism.

The thought itself is sacralized—spoken of as "a compass and spiritual food" of which "every word . . . is as good as ten thousand words." The writings of Chairman Mao become

> the best books in the world, the most scientific books, the most revolutionary books. . . . There have never been writings even in China or abroad like the writings of Chairman Mao. . . . They develop Marxism, Leninism, they are The Peak in the modern world of Marxism-Leninism. There are peaks in the mountains but the highest peak is called The Peak.

And this sacred quality of Maoist thought is in turn directly associated with the desired revolutionary totalism:

> One has to be totally revolutionary. There are total and non-total revolutionaries. Some men are like that. You cannot say they are not revolutionaries; but they are not

fully revolutionary. They are half revolutionary, half non-revolutionary. . . .

The total revolutionary, as the same passage goes on to explain, is "ready to sacrifice his life" and is (in paraphrase of Mao's own words) "not . . . afraid of wolves ahead and tigers behind . . . determined to change heaven and earth, fight the enemy, stick to the truth." Such dedication and courage are indeed possible insofar as one can genuinely worship Mao's thought along lines suggested by still another passage, which could well be viewed as the epitome of the immortalization of the word and all who embrace it:

> The thought of Mao Tse-tung is the sun in our heart, is the root of our life, is the source of all our strength. Through this, man becomes unselfish, daring, intelligent, able to do everything; he is not conquered by any difficulty and can conquer every enemy. The thought of Mao Tse-tung transforms man's ideology, transforms the Fatherland . . . through this the oppressed people of the world will rise.

The Maoist corpus is elevated to an all-consuming prophecy: it nurtures men, predicts their future, and changes the world to accomplish its own prediction; it sets in motion spiritual forces against which nothing can stand.
At times a hallowed thought sequence is suggested— from Marx to Mao, sometimes via Lenin and possibly Stalin, then continuing from Mao to Lin. Mao is said to have "creatively applied" Marx's thought and Lin to have done the same to Mao's—but the implication is that the first was a transformation achieved by a genius and the second

no more than the fidelity of a loyal disciple. The important thing is that the immortal corpus have continuity with past and future; that it be universal: "The light of the thoughts of Mao shines on the whole world." And that to resist it is tantamount to being annihilated: "To oppose the thought of Mao Tse-tung is to destroy oneself like a moth flying over a flame" (though one may add that since a moth tends to be drawn to a flame, the metaphor might also reflect an unspoken temptation to oppose the sacred thoughts).

This verbal genuflection before Mao has undoubtedly at times taken on qualities of tired ritual—a cliché for all occasions. And the staggering claims often made in the Chinese press for the application of these thoughts contribute to the instant ridicule with which they have been so widely greeted. Yet here again the matter bears closer scrutiny. The most famous target of ridicule was the insistence, early in the Cultural Revolution, that the thoughts of Mao had been responsible for China's brilliant successes in international table-tennis competition—and the mockery knew no bounds when the news came out later that the world champion himself had been strongly criticized for various shortcomings and eventually arrested. But M. Rufford Harrison, President of the United States Table Tennis Association, was considerably less derisive in his commentary:

> The writings and spirit of Mao invade every match the Chinese play. The national team, before beginning play, recite Mao quotations to give them courage and in the middle of a tense game a Chinese crowd will often chant Mao's sayings to spur their heroes on. It has a terrific psy-

chological effect, seeming to drive them to feats of endurance and other exceptional efforts.[6]

If we assume that Mr. Harrison speaks not as a Maoist but merely as an accurate observer, we are obliged to conclude that embracing the immortal corpus can indeed inspire unusual effort and accomplishment.

We may suspect similar combinations of ritualistic cliché and authenticity in widely disseminated claims of the marvelous contributions of Mao's thought to such large tasks as the drilling of oil wells, the construction of great modern airports, and the completion in record time of highly advanced and elaborate equipment for the steel industry. And when we are told how villagers, in true Maoist fashion, have "transformed heaven and earth" in achieving enormous victories over wind, sand, flood, and drought, there is no reason for us to doubt that some of the people involved in these projects felt energized by the Maoist phrases being chanted—any more than we would doubt that many who did not said that they did. Concerning the claim that Mao's thought was responsible for the unexpectedly early completion and successful testing of a hydrogen bomb (in June 1967), we have reason to believe that the major contribution of Maoism was to leave the nuclear scientists alone. But who is to say that none of them—and none of the technicians and soldiers later praised for their courageous achievements in entering the test area to evaluate the bomb's effects—were sustained at all by the death-defying Maoist images we have discussed? The slogan used on that occasion—"When men listen to this Chairman, machinery listens to men"—can become a dangerous simplification for a regime bent on industrialization. Indeed, as we shall soon observe, the entire Maoist program has foundered on it. All the same, men in a variety of situations could feel themselves strengthened by allying themselves to such an immortal corpus.

The procedure to be followed, as first applied in the Army and then throughout the country, was laid down by Lin Piao:

> Study [the Thought of Mao] with a question in mind; living study and living use; study and use combined. When use is urgent, study first, set up the stick and look at the shadow.

The "stick" of Mao's thought, in other words, sends off the "shadow" or guideline for the task at hand. Lin on another occasion spoke of the thought of Mao as "the great spiritual strength which will change into a great material force" —in itself a very Maoist way of viewing it. And whatever the purposeful use of such an image by Lin or its intrinsic exaggeration, we still do well to take the rhetoric seriously and recognize that the thought of any leader—certainly of this one—*is* convertible into material power, at least to a certain extent.

Highly instructive on the issue of psychological and physical benefits is an article by a military athlete entitled "The Power of Mao Tse-tung's Thought Is Infinite":

> For a time I suffered seriously from a nervous breakdown. My head ached in the daytime, I could not sleep at night, and I lacked energy. However, the thought of Mao

Tse-tung gave me unlimited strength. It gave me a greater courage to overcome difficulties. . . . I made great effort in study and training. With such strength I finally surmounted all difficulties, continually raised my technical level, and broke a number of national records.

The tone here seems to combine that of the religious convert and the enthusiastic beneficiary of psychotherapy. While religious converts backslide and psychiatric patients tend to modify initial enthusiasms, it is within the bounds of scientific possibility to assume that faith (trust) in the efficacy of Mao's thought—a sense of sharing in its immortalizing power—could have influences very much like those the athlete described. Evangelists and psychiatrists have done as much, one may claim, with a good deal less.

But it is in the nature of the Maoist corpus—child that it is of the excesses of the Cultural Revolution—to overstep itself and move toward an ideological abyss, as suggested in a statement by Lin Piao quoted before: "The best weapon of our troops is not the airplane, cannon, tank, or atomic bomb, but the thought of Mao Tse-tung; the greatest fighting force is the man armed with the thought of Mao Tse-tung, daring, not afraid of death." In the same spirit Mao's thought is said to articulate the "final struggle" between the world's "two major forces, revolution and counter-revolution." It is held to be the key to the "revolutionization of man," the inspiration for "the heroes [who] have aptly said: 'We must live for the people and die for the people . . . a revolutionary has no fear of death and one who fears death is no revolutionary.'" Now the message is: *so powerful has the immortal corpus rendered us that we become absolute conquerors of men, technology, and death.*

One might be tempted to dismiss the entire cult of Mao and his Thought as no more than sycophantic indulgence of an old man's vanity were it not for the life Mao has lived and the impact he has made upon the Chinese people. He has in fact come close to living out precisely the kind of existential absolute he has advocated. No twentieth-century life has come closer than his to the great myth of the hero—with its "road of trials," or prolonged death encounter, and its mastery of that encounter in a way that enhances the life of one's people.*

His message of mastery of death anxiety, reinforced by personal example, took on special relevance for a people living through a period (the first half of the twentieth century) in which such anxiety was continuously mobilized by extreme dislocation, violence, and loss. During such times there is always a hunger for words and acts that contribute to the re-ordering and "resymbolization" of collective existence.

At a more personal level we have noted Mao's preoccupation with his own series of survivals of intimate family members and revolutionary comrades. Mao's first wife and their son, his younger sister, and his two younger brothers all met violent deaths while serving the Chinese Commu-

---

* I have elsewhere suggested [7] that this theme of conquering death is more central to the myth of the hero than is the Oedipus complex, which Freud and other early psychoanalytic writers saw as the key to the myth.

nist movement. Mao lost his last sibling when his brother
Mao Tse-min was executed in 1943 by a warlord (who had
suddenly switched allegiance from the Communists to the
Nationalists); and since he had actively guided and directed his brother's revolutionary career, this death must
have engendered in him especially strong feelings of what
I have elsewhere called guilt over survival priority. There
is much evidence that Mao felt very strongly not only
about these losses but about the manner in which they occurred. He has frequently revealed unusual sensitivity to
death imagery in general and to survivor guilt in particular. But rather than being incapacitated by such feelings,
he has, in the manner of all great leaders, applied them to
the larger historical crises of his day. *

---

* Significantly, two of the "three constantly read articles" so in-
tensively focused upon during the Cultural Revolution were written
in commemoration of individual deaths. "Serve the People" was
originally a speech delivered by Mao at a memorial meeting for
Chang Szu-teh, a soldier of the Guard Regiment of the Central
Committee of the Chinese Communist Party; and in the essay Mao
uses this soldier's death as a prototype for the general principle of
dying for an immortal cause. "In Memory of Norman Bethune" was
written only about five weeks after the death of the Canadian surgeon.
And the third essay, while not specifically commemorative, has direct bearing on issues of symbolic immortality. It is entitled "The
Foolish Old Man Who Removed the Mountains" (in its original
version "How Yu Kung Removed the Mountains"), and it takes from
Chinese folklore the story of an old man of North China who, because the way from his house was obstructed by two great mountains, "with great determination . . . led his sons in digging up the
mountains, hoe in hand." When told he was foolish he replied:
"When I die, my sons will carry on; when they die, there will be
my grandsons, and then their sons and grandsons, and so on to infinity . . . why can't we dig [the mountains] away?" Finally "God

One could draw upon a number of illustrative examples. For instance, in 1919, when Mao was still a little-known apprentice revolutionary editing a periodical in Changsha (the capital of Hunan province), a young girl of that city, whose parents had forced her to marry against her will, committed suicide. Mao was sufficiently moved by the incident to write nine newspaper articles in thirteen days denouncing the old society's restrictions upon individual liberty and anticipating a future "great wave of the freedom to love." Leaving aside the historical irony of his own later imposition of restrictions in many ways greater than those he condemned as a young libertarian, we note his unusually strong reaction to an individual death. Here and on other occasions he could embrace a form of death guilt that could be put to social use. We may speak of this as an *activist response to death*—whether the death be of an immediate biological kind (as in this case) or of the more symbolic kind exemplified by chaos and injustice. The necessary combination for this response is full openness to death anxiety and death guilt, and an immediate transcendence of these emotions through linking them directly

---

was moved . . . and he sent down two angels, who carried the mountains away on their backs." Mao goes on to say that imperialism and feudalism are "two big mountains [lying] like a dead weight on the Chinese people," and that "Our God is none other than the masses of the Chinese people." Though the speech was given in 1945 when Mao was in his early fifties and by no means an "old man," it is a perfect parable of both revolutionary immortality and Mao's own involvement in the quest. (The version I quote is from the *Peking Review* of March 17,1967, and differs from the original in a number of ways, notably in the revised stress upon the old man's "foolishness" when judged according to conventional wisdom.)

to revolutionary struggles. And without attempting to detail Mao's remarkable achievements, we may say that this combination has greatly contributed to his *revitalizing talents* as a peasant organizer, military strategist, Party leader, head of state, and general theorist in the "sinification" of Marxism.

Mao's relationship to the myth of the hero is also enhanced by certain qualities of personal and revolutionary style that reveal a man closely attuned to the pulse of immortality. One such trait is his celebrated "revolutionary romanticism," a designation which would sound highly derogatory to most communist ears but which official Chinese commentaries have associated with courage in the face of objective difficulties, and with great revolutionary vision (to be distinguished, of course, from *non*-revolutionary romanticism, regarded as an unrealistic expression of philosophical idealism).* The image of the revolutionary romanticist has been fostered by Mao's series of brilliantly conducted guerrilla campaigns during the twenties and thirties and by his writings about these campaigns; by his continuing combination of "guerrilla ethos" and "heaven-storming" approach to the transformation of Chinese society, combining heroic effort with extreme auster-

---

* One commentary, published in 1961, speaks of the two sides of revolutionary romanticism, "its romantic spirit and its romantic method." The former "lies in seeing what is new in life, reflecting it with success, helping it to grow," and the latter includes literary use of "exaggeration, . . . flights of fancy, and mythological coloration." But also stressed is the "synthesis of revolutionary realism and revolutionary romanticism." The Chinese term for romanticism, *lang-man chu-i,* was adapted from Western usage and has a similar connotation to that of the English counterpart.[8]

ity (on the order of the old slogan of "millet plus rifles");
and by his general affinity for outlaws, and for the romantic aura often bestowed by Chinese tradition upon outlaws
as noble subverters of prevailing social evil. For such reasons a Chinese writer once called Mao "fundamentally a
character from a Chinese novel or opera." And Stuart
Schram speaks of his "military romanticism," by which he
means Mao's tendency to "regard war as the supreme
adventure and the supreme test of human courage and human will," along with a "warlike quality of his tempera-
ment and imagination [which leads him to] post economic and even scientific and philosophical problems in
these terms." [9] *Mao's revolutionary romanticism, then, is
the hero's quest for doing more than the possible, risking
and even courting death in order to alter the meaning of
both life and death, "storming heaven" and challenging
the claims of existing deities, political as well as theological, in order to replace them with the claims of revolutionary immortality.* Associated with this romantic affinity
for transcendence have been some of Mao's greatest

* Mao frequently impressed others as a man with a heroic mission.
On the basis of their 1936 meeting, Snow wrote: "undeniably you
feel a certain force of destiny in him . . . nothing quick or flashy,
but a kind of solid elemental vitality," and "Mao Tse-tung may possibly become a very great man." Snow's further comments touched
upon the hero's capacity to conquer death: "Mao has the reputation
of a charmed life. He has been repeatedly pronounced dead by Nan-
king, only to return to the news columns a few days later, as active as
ever . . . there seems to be some basis for the legend of his
charmed life, however, in the fact that, although he has been in
scores of battles, was once captured by enemy troops and escaped,
and has had the world's highest reward on his head, during all of
these years he has never once been wounded." [10]

achievements (the Communist victory itself and the revitalization of China) as well as his most spectacular failures (the Great Leap Forward and perhaps the Cultural Revolution).

A closely related psychological and historical pattern is his extreme identification with—or what has been called his "mystical faith" in—the Chinese rural masses. Some observers have attributed this simply to Mao's own peasant background, but in 1936 Edgar Snow noted a combination of peasantlike qualities ("simplicity and naturalness . . . plain-speaking and plain-living . . . some people might think him rather coarse and vulgar") and "the most incisive wit and worldly sophistication." [11] Mao's relationship to his peasant background is undoubtedly more complex than usually recognized. Having rebelled against a father who had himself risen from a poor-peasant to a "middle-" or "rich-peasant" category, we may suspect that Mao's passionate glorification of the peasant state permitted him to channel ambivalent emotions of affection and resentment toward that state into a formulation that was both revolutionary and "Chinese." In any case, he perceived very early the special significance of "peasant power" for Chinese Communism and for the country's future. In the process he evolved an identification that rooted him firmly in China's cultural and racial substance, and a quality of concern for her national destiny even to the point of marked Sinocentrism.

From the time of his youth Mao has resisted numerous opportunities to travel abroad, and it is nothing less than extraordinary that during his long life he has spent only a total of about one month away from Chinese soil, during two brief trips to Moscow in 1949 and 1957.* Many have noted the political significance of his lifelong concern with Chinese dignity. The nature of this preoccupation is strikingly revealed in a few seemingly inconsequential vignettes recorded by Schram: Mao as a young man in Shanghai in 1924, dressed in old Chinese clothes, coming across a former schoolmate dressed in Western style whom he promptly tells to change his suit, and when asked why says, "I'll show you" and leads his friend to the infamous sign in a nearby park, "Chinese and Dogs Not Allowed"; Mao at an even earlier age as a spectator at a soccer game in which one of the contestants was Yale-in-China (a secondary school attended by youths from privileged families with Western connections) suddenly rising from the crowd and shouting "Beat the slaves of foreigners!"; Mao the scatological lyricist (in this and some other ways reminding one of Martin Luther) denouncing the Chinese government's subservience to the West with the pithy observation, "If one of our foreign masters farts, it's a lovely perfume."

It becomes clear that from the time of his youth Mao has felt himself deeply involved in a struggle to restore national pride—which over the years became nothing less than a heroic quest to reassert the life power of China. Hence, Mao came to associate communism with the timeless virtues of the peasant masses and of the Chinese earth. And his relentless pursuit of the thought reform process

---

* In marked contrast, most prominent Asian revolutionaries of his generation spent years abroad during which, in many cases, their political visions, attitudes toward the West, and personal identities were significantly shaped.

has been an effort to cement this association, especially within the minds of intellectuals. Mao once described his Communist movement as "passionately concerned with the fate of the Chinese nation, and moreover with its fate throughout all eternity." [12] And one recalls Mao's ringing declaration, upon his victorious assumption of power in 1949, that China had "stood up" and would "never again be an insulted nation"—an expression of national resurgence which was as authentically Maoist as it was Chinese. *Rather than speak of Mao as a "father figure" or "mother figure" for his countrymen (no doubt he has been both), we do better to see him as a death-conquering hero who became the embodiment of Chinese immortality.*

Mao himself seems to experience inwardly this heroic fusion of man and nature in his special style of historical preoccupation—a mythical cast of thought within which (as Mark Gayn explains) "the great men and the villains of the past were familiar and contemporary, and . . . what was happening now was indeed a natural sequel to a much older drama." So much so that one was left with the feeling that "history was [Mao's] habitat, from the first Chinese dynasty on, and that he felt close kinship to all the great rebels of the past." [13]* [Only such a singular capacity to identify himself with Chinese cultural and historical substance could have led Mao to pursue the outrageous extremes of the Cultural Revolution.] It is as if he were attempting to establish the conviction that China's heroic dimensions—her great history, vast land, stagger-

* This tendency to bestow upon the distant past great psychological force and immediacy is to some extent a Chinese cultural trait, but one apparently present in Mao to an unusual degree.

ing population, and legendary revolution—render her im-
mune to the dangers of the contemporary world and to the
limitations of human existence.

Mao's "romantic" channels to immortality are nowhere
more in evidence than in his special way with words.
While he can at times be as mundane as any other propa-
gandist, and the rhetoric *about* him can be worse than
that, there is no denying his talent for the reverberating
phrase. This often takes the form of the especially apt use
of a Chinese folk saying, as in the case of his by now famous slogan, "The east wind prevails over the west wind."
When he first uttered the phrase in Moscow in 1957, he
was understood to mean the political East or the socialist
camp, and only later did it come to signify the geographical and racial East. But there can be little doubt that the
second set of meanings was present at least potentially
from the beginning, and that at some psychic level "east
wind" referred to Chinese cultural-revolutionary substance. The impact of the metaphor is further enhanced
and generalized by its suggestion of eternal nature, so that
other non-Western countries can claim it as their own.

We encounter a similar affinity for images of immortality in his poetry. Our concern is less with the question of
literary merit than with the use of a literary medium for
asserting modes of transcendence.

One poem, written in 1957, actually bears the title "The
Immortals." [14] It was composed in response to another
poem sent to him by a widow who had lost her husband, a

close revolutionary comrade of Mao's, in battle twenty-five years before. In it Mao reveals his articulate sensitivity to death guilt by commemorating both the dead comrade and his own wife, who had been executed by the Kuomintang in 1930. The first two lines—"I lost my proud poplar, and you your willow,/Poplar and willow soar lightly to the heaven of heavens"—suggest the immortalization of the two revolutionary martyrs. The poem goes on to describe how the two are presented "respectfully with cassia wine" by Wu Kang, a legendary figure said to have sought immortality so intensely that he committed certain crimes in the process, and was therefore condemned for eternity to the Sisyphian task of chopping down a tree which would immediately become whole again each time it was severed. The suggestion of heavenly wine contrasts with an undercurrent of ultimate futility concerning the quest for immortality and of guilt over methods used in the quest. One suspects that this is an unconscious revelation of an aspect of Mao's own psychological state at that time. In any case the poem's message emerges in its last four lines:

> The lonely goddess in the moon spreads her ample sleeves
> To dance for these faithful souls in the endless sky.
> Of a sudden comes word of the tiger's defeat on earth,
> And they break into tears of torrential rain.

The tiger (we are told by official interpreters) refers to the Kuomintang regime; and the "tears of torrential rain" express the joy of the two martyrs at the enemy's defeat. The two are now clearly immortals, and the poem is a highly romantic but specific formulation that renders their deaths significant by associating them with revolutionary triumph decades later.

Mao's poetry also reveals his capacity to reach back to his psychological roots for the reassertion of an immortal vision. Thus, a poem written in June 1959—when grave national problems coincided with his personal defeats—describes his impressions upon returning to his native village and recalling the peasant movement he had led there thirty-two years earlier. The last half of the poem summarizes its theme:

> Only because so many sacrificed themselves did our wills become strong,
> So that we dared command the sun and moon to bring a new day.
> I love to look at the multiple waves of rice and beans,
> While on every side the heroes return through the evening haze.

The heroes in the last line are peasants returning from work; the immortal Chinese substance they represent blends with an earlier revolutionary combination of sacrifice and omnipotent power that could "command the sun and moon to bring a new day." In a poem written in 1962 Mao expresses similar sentiments: "Only the hero dares to pursue the tiger,/Still less does any brave fellow fear the bear." The animal references are to the "paper tiger" of imperialism and to the Russian bear. And once more these exultant images were expressed at a time when Mao must certainly have felt himself threatened by a variety of enemies near and far. For him the moment of greatest danger

—when one is closest to defeat and extinction—is the moment of greatest opportunity for heroic transcendence and revitalization.

Mao's romantic imagery of transcendence is again evident in a 1961 poem that tells how the poet "would dream a dream" in which he could "see the Land of the Hibiscus wholly illuminated by the light of dawn." The Land of the Hibiscus is a literary name for his native Hunan province, and could in this poem refer to China in general, or even to the entire world becoming a revolutionary Promised Land of virtue and light. Finally, in a poem written in 1963, containing what Schram refers to as "an extraordinary mixture of revolutionary and traditional imagery which epitomizes the whole of [Mao's] thought and action," we can observe the combination of power and destructiveness this entails:

On our tiny globe
A few flies smash into the walls,
They buzz,
Some loudly complaining,
Others weeping.
The ants climb the flowering locust, boasting of their
    great country
But for ants to shake a tree is easier said than done.
Just now the west wind drops leaves on Ch'angan,
Whistling arrows fly through the air.

How many urgent tasks
Have arisen one after the other!
Heaven and earth revolve,
Time presses,
Ten thousand years is too long,
We must seize the day.

The four seas rise high, the clouds and the waters rage,
The five continents tremble, wind and thunder are unleashed,
We must sweep away all the harmful insects
Until not a single enemy remains.

Official commentaries are again helpful. The world becomes tiny for the genuine revolutionary capable of transforming it by his action; the flies represent imperialism or
modern revisionism, hurling themselves against the
"walls" of true Marxism-Leninism; the ants are the Soviets; the leaves dropped by the west wind are reactionary
forces in general; and Ch'angan, the ancient capital, is
China. The "whistling arrows" are Marxist-Leninist truth,
and the ants who "climb the flowering locust, boasting of
their great country" refer both to insectlike Soviets and to
a T'ang dynasty legend of a man who dreamt he visited
the country of the Great Flowering Locust Tree to receive
great honors there, only to discover on awakening the reality behind the dream, an anthill at the foot of a locust tree
outside his window.

The combination of traditional and revolutionary imagery Schram speaks of, then, reflects precisely the capacity
we have repeatedly observed in Mao to create an immortal
vision compounded of both revolutionary and Chinese
cultural-racial themes. The vision includes the annihilation of helpless and self-deceiving adversaries. When the
poem was written (1963) the matter was urgent in the
extreme ("Time presses,/Ten thousand years is too long,/
We must seize the day"). Rather than a smooth and beautiful transcendence, all is "wind and thunder." And the demand to "sweep away all of the harmful insects,/Until not
a single enemy remains" is a peal of totalism, an image of

Armageddon containing the most malignant aspects of the power-purity constellation.

It has often been said that a historical innovator manages to interpret the most fundamental experiences of his generation. Such experiences inevitably involve coping with death and achieving symbolic immortality; we may say that Mao has done precisely that, always with an impulse toward the transcendent, and not only for his own generation. His accomplishments and inclinations rendered him a likely candidate for the excesses of virtue with which the Cultural Revolution was to anoint him.

Over the course of Mao's later career the word becomes not only flesh but *his* flesh. The man-word corpus is increasingly represented as *absolutely* identical with China's destiny. And we sense that we are witnessing the *tragic transition from the great leader to the despot.*

Mao's active participation in the creation of his own cult has become increasingly clear. His rewriting of earlier works—in order, as Schram says, "to remove both youthful errors and any points of fact or doctrine which did not suit the current orthodoxy"—is consistent with practices of other modern Communist leaders, and also with those of pre-modern Chinese Emperors in the process of enthroning themselves and establishing new dynasties. But Mao seems to go further than anyone else in the infusion of his man-word corpus into every psychological cranny of Chinese existence. So involved has he become with the principle of the cult of the leader that much of his anger toward Khrushchev was believed to be bound up

with the latter's policy of de-Stalinization and accompanying theoretical attack upon the "cult of personality" in
general. Thus, when Edgar Snow observed (during his
1965 interview with Mao) that China had been criticized
for fostering such a cult, Mao admitted that "perhaps
there was some." Mao then pointed out that Stalin had
been the center of a cult of personality, and asked in
turn whether it was possible that Khrushchev fell "because
he had no cult of personality at all."

Mao apparently requires the immortalizing corpus for
his "romantic" sense of self and history, his image of heroic
confrontation with the powers of heaven and earth. The
extremities of the deification would seem to confirm his
highly active complicity in the process, and his loss of perspective concerning its wider impact. One thinks of the
shock and disgust of Eastern European audiences when
reviewing dramatic performances by visiting Chinese
troupes in which the image of Mao became almost liter-
ally a deity. And of incidents such as the reported comment of an old Uighur from Sinkiang, upon shaking hands
with Mao: "In the past we . . . greeted each other wish-
ing, Huta [God] protect you; today we have changed this
into the Party protect you, Chairman Mao protect you."
One thinks too of the remarkable feat of physical endurance Mao is alleged to have demonstrated on July 16,
1966, at the age of seventy-two, in a nine-mile swim down
the Yangtze in the extraordinary time of sixty-five minutes,
despite stopping at one point to teach a young woman the

backstroke. The attendant stress upon "Chairman Mao's good health and long life" seemed to make him into a kind of legendary hero who had achieved something close to physical omnipotence and immortality of the flesh.* And most significant of all has been the godlike style of Mao's participation in public events—such as the great Red Guard rally of August 18, 1966, at which he emerged at sunrise, a silent divinity who witnessed everything and by his mere presence conferred upon hundreds of thousands (on other occasions, millions) of young people a sense of being reawakened in purity—much in the manner of an Indian Holy Man who need only make an appearance before ordinary people to transmit his godlike power to them.

But the great leader turns into a despot when he loses confidence in his claim to immortality. Then, feeling himself threatened by biological and symbolic death, he becomes obsessed with survival as such. He is no longer able to put his death guilt effectively in the service of a noble mission, and instead becomes an "eternal survivor" who requires the defeat or death of a never-ending series of "enemies" in order to reactivate his own life and revive his ever faltering sense of immortality. We may then suspect

* The event was filmed, but some observers are convinced that the Chinese employed a "double" for Mao; or if not, that they falsified such things as the length of the swim and the time in which it was achieved, and neglected to mention the Yangtze's strong current, which could be a factor in carrying a swimmer rapidly over a considerable distance. Whatever the manipulations involved, the purpose of the swim was to demonstrate Mao's vigor following what was admitted to have been a long illness.

that he depends heavily upon the mechanism of denial—upon the fantasy "I am *not* losing my power, I am *not* dying." He resorts to ever more desperate and magical efforts at achieving vitality. Since no one can provide the power over death that is sought, all become enemies, and we begin to observe something close to the Caligula-like state I have described elsewhere[16] as "survivor paranoia." *

Also involved is an old man's fear that he is losing his "potency." In speaking of the potency of a great revolutionary, I refer by no means only to his sexual capacity or physical strength, but to the special power of one who has felt himself to be a transmitter of forces shaping the destiny of mankind. Here it is instructive to compare Mao with Gandhi. We may say that in old age both experienced this sense of declining power, and that both sought to revitalize themselves through reassertion of purity. In Gandhi's case that purity took the form of a *personal* demonstration of control: his sleeping with naked young girls as a form of experiment with temptation and exercise in sexual restraint. Both men sought to buttress a relationship to the eternal by calling upon the purity and life power of the young. But where Gandhi looked upon this aspect of his struggle as a private discipline, Mao enlarged his quest for purity to include the whole of China and

* I am not suggesting that Mao is mad, nor am I making a clinical psychiatric diagnosis of any kind; there is no convincing evidence for such a diagnosis. Moreover, one must be very cautious about applying individual psychopathological terms to collective behavior. What I am suggesting (by the term "survivor paranoia") as possibly relevant to Mao is a state of mind affecting aging leaders after long and repeated survivorlike crises in which there can be certain paranoid contours.

staked the future of an entire revolution upon it. This is not to suggest that the Cultural Revolution is a product merely of Mao's intrapsychic struggles; but rather that such inner struggles now spread confusion and antagonism, rather than the illumination they had in the past. Thus threatened by loss of personal and revolutionary power, the bold stroke of a leader's genius becomes the despotic turbulence of an eternal survivor.[17]

In classical psychoanalytic terms one could view the entire process as "the death of the father"—the aging leader's reluctance to permit the inevitable ascendancy of his assertive "sons." But it may be more accurate to speak of it as "the death of the word." The capacity of the revolutionary-Maoist combination of words and images to mediate between inner and outer worlds is, at least temporarily, moribund. Hence Mao's plunge into psychism, into a one-sided focus upon intrapsychic purity at the expense of extrapsychic reality. In place of his formerly sensitive application of personal passions to China's desperate historical experience, we encounter instead a misplaced faith in his own psychic state—a substitution of his own psychic history for history at large. Because he and a few around him fear the death of the revolution, China must be made to convulse.

In this psychism there remains a combined vision of noble aspiration and total manipulation—as vividly revealed in a statement Mao made in 1958 during the Great Leap Forward:

Apart from their other characteristics, China's 600 million people have two remarkable peculiarities: they are, first of all, poor, and secondly blank. That may seem like a bad thing. But it is really a good thing. Poor people want change, want to do things, want revolution. A clean sheet of paper has no blotches, and so the newest and most beautiful words can be written on it, the newest and most beautiful pictures can be painted on it.

Each Chinese—really man himself—is a *tabula rasa,* a "clean sheet of paper" upon which *anything* can be written. By imprinting upon his mind "the newest and most beautiful words" and "the newest and most beautiful pictures," all problems of the inner and outer worlds can be solved.

One thinks of Mao in his Yenan cave, his view of the world symbolized by the sparse contents of his "rickety bookcase"—mainly Chinese classics and the works of Marx and Lenin—and one can imagine how, in times of crisis, he would make a spiritual return to that magnificent isolation and seek to impose his heroic purities upon all of his countrymen.*

---

* The image is partly metaphorical. Mao's reading was by no means limited to Chinese classics and Marx and Lenin. Moreover, Yenan was at that time a busy small city with activities of every kind and a considerable number of visitors from various parts of the world. Yet Mao did live in a cave (or what Gunther Stein called a "four-cave 'apartment' " just outside the town; it was "whitewashed and sparsely furnished" (Stein also mentions a "rickety chair"), and (according to Evans Carlson) Mao worked at night by the pale light of "a single candle." More important was the state of mind developed in Yenan and other geographically obscure communist sanctuaries— what Benjamin Schwartz speaks of as an "image of . . . society as

This is the true meaning of the "Yenan complex." It is also the essence of psychism. The leader turns inward toward an increasingly idiosyncratic and extreme vision of immortality, and demands that his vision be permanently imprinted upon all. Mao's actions belie his stated willingness to leave assessments of present revolutionary developments to future generations. As much as any leader in recent centuries he seeks to chart and control history and "fix its course for centuries to come." [19] The more resistance to this course he encounters among the living, the more he looks toward the infinity of the future and seeks vindication from the unborn.

---

an armed camp of comrades-in-arms, united in clear-cut conflict against the ubiquitous reactionary enemy." [18]

VII

TECHNOLOGY
AND PSYCHISM

THE PHENOMENON of psychism, then, is a key to the limitations of the Maoist vision. And psychism is intimately bound up with technology—with the distinction man must make between self and things, between mind and its material products.

Man has been struggling with this distinction since he fashioned his first tool, and the evolution of the modern world is closely tied up with it. But the distinction has never been complete. Nor perhaps can it, since we perceive external things only by means of internal—or mental—forms; so that there is a sense in which the only significance technology can have for us lies in the images we create around it. The problem is heightened by the overwhelming "presence" of twentieth-century things, and the increasing psychic tendency for man to re-create himself according to a technological model. It is further compounded by the polar ambivalence felt by contemporary man for technology, on the one hand a source of liberation from poverty and oppression, on the other a means of total annihilation.

In this sense China's struggles with technology are part

of a vast confusion that envelops the entire planet. But her struggles are intensified by her relatively backward position within a series of keenly felt rivalries—with the more "developed" countries, with the white West, and with the Soviet Union. There is a strong Chinese feeling that technology can be a route to the recovery of past cultural glory. Hence, Mao's hunger for technology, together with his insistence that it be acquired on his own spiritual terms, can be seen as the latest episode in China's hundred-year struggle to cope with the modern world according to the unworkable principle of grafting alien Western knowledge and technique onto an immutably Chinese "essence."

We are not surprised that psychism of various kinds emerged very strongly during the movement epitomizing Mao's confrontation with technology, the Great Leap Forward. The "beautiful words" and "beautiful pictures" he then envisioned being written and painted on a "blank" Chinese people were words and pictures of rapid technological achievement. His assumption was that China "might not need as much time as previously thought to catch up with the big capitalist countries in industrial and agricultural production." Equally significant was the simultaneous emergence of the slogan of the "uninterrupted" or "permanent" revolution, a slogan which can be understood as an ideological call to revolutionary immortality, and which paved the way for the Cultural Revolution.

The methods of the Great Leap Forward, to be sure, had a compelling external logic: putting into use the human labor with which rural China abounds as a substitute for the large machinery she lacks, and thereby creating both national and local self-sufficiency, or, as the official slogan had it, "walking with two legs." But it turned out that the "legs" were largely psychic, and while psychic legs are of the greatest importance, they cannot substitute for either bodily or technological ones—especially in the making of steel. Underlying this logic, then, was a quality of feeling that Schurmann and Schell describe as "magnificent madness":

> From early 1958 on, all of China was in a fever pitch of work. Everywhere backyard steel furnaces were erected;* roads, dams, reservoirs, small-scale factories were built. Steel, symbol of Stalin's industrialization, had been the preserve of a few modern plants; now everyone could make his own steel. Just as the masses were the foundations of politics, now they would become the foundation of the economy. . . .
>
> As the organized masses hurled themselves into the front line of production, their cadre leaders became dizzy with success. As products rolled out of the factories and production figures climbed, the cadres felt that for years they had been subject to a gigantic swindle which they called the fetishism of technology. Industrial work was not so complicated as the educated technicians had told them. Who needed complex blueprints when a single drawing sufficed? Economists had told them they must keep careful records. Why, when a few figures were enough to tell the planners what the masses were doing. In any case, the need for planners was not so great any longer. Planning work was sitting in offices, and that was bureaucratism. The state would soon wither away, the cadres were told, and so thousands of trained economists were fired from their jobs.[1]

* These backyard furnaces were actually for the smelting of pig-iron.

The magnificence lay in a vision of vast technological transformation achieved by and for ordinary unspecialized human beings. The madness lay in the assumption that one could ignore the intellectual and mechanical requirements of technology and depend instead upon human will.

The backyard furnace became a symbol (certainly for the outside world, and, one suspects, for Chinese as well) of the topsy-turvy world of the Great Leap: at first a source of wonder as it appeared where no furnace had ever been, heralding exciting innovations in production by "the people," and then "dissolve [ing] into piles of mud and brick after a few rains." [2] The movement was by no means a complete failure: some production notably increased, useful small industries were developed, and various forms of valuable experience were gained. But on the whole the country was left in profound economic disorder, a large percentage of its plants and factories functioning erratically, without statistical control or standardization, and in many cases having to be abandoned entirely.

What precisely was the fallacy? Mark Gayn sees it as the "premise . . . that it was possible to build a twentieth-century industry atop a countryside still barely emerging from the eighteenth," and also points out that "the village was given verbal honors—and a low budgetary appropriation." [3] In other words, under the guise of village-centered purity actual village life was neglected in favor of a kind of "instant technology." The same principle seemed to apply in the vast program of "people's communes" undertaken in conjunction with the Great Leap, and with equally disastrous results. Here too there was a magnificent vision, but one of "naïve utopianism," [4] as expressed in a poem composed by peasants during the summer of 1958 in the midst of the campaign:

> Setting up a people's commune is like going to heaven,
> The achievements of a single night surpass those of several
> millennia
> The sharp knife severs the roots of private property
> Opening a new historical era.

What becomes clear in examining the entire tone of the Great Leap is *the extent to which the passions behind the vision of immortal Chinese revolutionary and cultural substance took precedence over accurate perception of the environment and of the requirements for altering it.* Kang Chao describes how this worked:

> Under the slogans "politics takes command" and "reliance on the mass line," the administrative system within an enterprise underwent considerable disruption. Technicians and engineers were humiliated by the existence of a situation under which experts had to listen to non-experts in technical matters, scientific laws were replaced by political demands, and production fell into the hands of a group of "fanatics." [5]

Here we see in operation the Maoist assumption that "revolutionary enthusiasm and ideological purity could make up for the lack of technical competence and material means." [6] We are dealing then with a *psychistic fallacy,* an assumption of the interchangeability of psychic state and technology. *Technology is sought but feelings are cultivated.* *

* Certain Chinese cultural patterns have long encouraged tendencies

The feeling-state can, in fact, become the entire operative universe—as suggested by the following commentary on Mao's thought, also written at the time of the Great Leap:

> Many living examples show that *there is only unproductive thought, there are no unproductive regions*. There are only poor methods for cultivating the land, there is no such thing as poor land. Provided only that people manifest in full measure their subjective capacities for action, it is possible to modify natural conditions.[8]

---

toward psychism. Mary Wright [7] has described conflicts during the nineteenth century between the Confucian stress upon moral training as the sole requirement for the governing of men and modern efforts to supplement such training with knowledge of foreign languages, mathematics, and science. These nineteenth-century conflicts resemble later Communist "Red versus expert" controversies, just as the traditional military motto "The conduct of war rests with men, not with implements" anticipates later Maoist attitudes. Thus a leading conservative philosopher-official of that time said: ". . . as the mind dominates nature, so the quality of the officials decides the fate of the Empire." And behind such Confucian (and neo-Confucian) attitudes were more extreme assumptions that "nature and morality are mutually dependent," so that drought and flood were believed to be caused by insufficient sincerity and frugality on the part of officials. Such notions of natural disaster resulting from failure to follow culturally prescribed rules are common in many primitive and peasant societies, but as Mary Wright also points out, they have "nowhere else developed into a governing principle of a long-lived empire." There is, in other words, a Chinese tradition for approaching crises of politics, technology, and nature almost exclusively by means of psychic cultivation. And like Mao (if not quite to his extreme) traditional philosophers beginning with Confucius and Mencius have stressed the malleability and teachability of men.

"Unproductive thought" can of course refer to lack of intellectual initiative, but it is much more likely to refer to a psychic level of revolutionary enthusiasm. And that psychic state becomes interchangeable not only with technology but with nature itself. There is no external world, only a struggle for internal perfection. Subjected to intense methods of psychological influence, an entire nation is asked to treat the physical universe as if it were nothing but feeling and will. In the process of attempting to subjugate technology and nature to human control (or "to subjective capacities"), their material actuality is denied. *

The consequences of this psychistic fallacy could not remain hidden; they have in fact been a major cause of opposition to Mao among formerly loyal followers. For those who simply attended to the self-evident truth that some land was fertile and other land poor, whatever the "subjective capacities" of the cultivators—and who could distinguish between a steel mill (or pig-iron smelter) and a crude *idea* of one—became the Party "pragmatists" so quickly numbered among his enemies. Thus, although Liu publicly supported the Great Leap Forward in Mao's name (though he might well have had reservations about it), the definitive break between the two men apparently occurred over the extreme measures adopted at Mao's insistance during the course of the program, and over the

---

* At the same time there has occurred in China the opposite but related kind of confusion between mental life and technology mentioned before as existing in the West: the technologized self-image contained in the demand that each person become a "stainless screw" in the "locomotive of revolution."

subsequent liberalization under Liu's leadership as a means of recovery. The psychological and socioeconomic reverberations of the Great Leap are undoubtedly still being felt in China, and one might view the Cultural Revolution itself as a kind of "second Leap" in response to a Maoist need to vindicate the first one. Motivated in part by the urge to outdo Russian and Chinese ideological rivals, the Great Leap Forward was an extraordinarily bold plunge into the communist future. Yet in its reliance upon a psychistic conception of reality, it had a dreamlike premodern, even prehistorical aura.

But after one has said this one must recognize aspects of Chinese Communist historical experience in which "revolutionary will" did indeed appear to serve as a substitute for technology—experiences which almost take the fallacy out of the psychistic fallacy. One need only recall the extraordinary success of guerrilla troops during the early days of the revolution in arming themselves with their opponents' weapons. Mao told Edgar Snow in 1965 that the Chinese revolution, rather than being engineered by the Russians as many claimed, was "in truth . . . armed by Americans." He referred not only to the American-made guns captured from American-trained Nationalist Chinese soldiers, but to the recruiting of these soldiers in one way or another to the Communist side—a process known in the colorful Chinese vernacular as "changing of hats." Eyewitness reports—such as Derk Bodde's—of the Liberation Army's entry into Peking in 1949 tend to confirm Mao's version of things:

. . . I counted over 250 heavy motor vehicles of all kinds —tanks, armored cars, truckloads of soldiers, trucks mounted with machine guns, trucks towing heavy artillery. Behind them followed innumerable ambulances, jeeps, and other smaller vehicles. As probably the greatest demonstration of Chinese military might in history, the spectacle was enormously impressive. But what made it especially memorable to Americans was the fact that it was primarily a display of *American* military equipment, virtually all of it captured or obtained by bribe from Kuomintang forces in the short space of two and one-half years.[9]

We may think of such a process as a kind of "technological judo," a means of putting to effective use one's opponent's technological strength. "Revolutionary will" was crucial, but as a means of obtaining—not replacing—the necessary military technology. What was involved at the time, therefore, was by no means psychism. The weapons were presumably manufactured in an American environment, which took full heed of technological requirements, and the Chinese Red Army itself placed the highest value upon these weapons. But the nostalgic attempt to use this kind of experience as a model for very different and much more complex contemporary social and economic situations has encouraged the psychism we have been discussing.

For technological judo no longer suffices. Among other things it requires excessive dependency upon one's opponents: one needs them to draw upon their strength. The process in fact comes close to realizing the principle of "Chinese essence, Western technique" mentioned earlier. But as the Chinese have so painfully learned, the first is not unaffected by the second, and true autonomy requires creating one's own "techniques." At a certain point, therefore, one must face the actualities of one's own technological struggles.

One is then forced to learn what is for an extreme voluntarist the most difficult of lessons: rather than the psychic state replacing technology, technology profoundly modifies the psychic state. Instead of being able to "treat capital formation as a type of guerrilla warfare," the process of capital formation and accompanying technological development tends to undermine precisely that guerrilla ethos. Maoists have resisted the general recognition of the degree to which people are altered by industrialization. And as Mark Gayn comments, "when, in consternation, they discovered that yesterday's peasants—and especially the peasants' sons—have become a changed breed, the leaders began to demand that the new urbanites return to the country to rediscover its virtues and its patterns of thought." [10] Here is the familiar model of peasant purity. The psychistic fallacy is the assumption on the part of any senior group that it can instill in the young the "old virtues"—that some form of imposed psychic experience could eliminate all of the very elements in the environment which discouraged those "old virtues" in favor of newer ones.

Moreover, an environment concentrating upon scientific and technological development tends to produce men who ask questions about results. One young man I spoke to in Hong Kong, who had left China during the period of the Great Leap after years of devoted work as a Party cadre, noted the contrast between the meager material state of the people and the extravagant technological visions put forth by the regime. His comment was, "If the Party's interpretations of things were true, one year of their reconstruction should have been the equivalent of twenty years of anybody else's." And his question: "Why do they have to put intellectuals through so much reform to convince them of this?" Here we observe the emergence of what is sometimes called "the scientific intellectual"—a man who may be as prone to irrationality as his historical predecessors but who is at least inclined to approach his projects with a certain amount of systematic thought and his surroundings with a measure of pragmatism. If not always a completely reliable guide, he does on the whole make the distinction between psychic state and technology. Indeed, he is committed to the reality of technology—whether by occupation (as a scientist), by general cast of mind (a concern with intellectual "technique" or "methodology"), or even at times by opposition to the excesses of that technology. And he is absolutely essential to any modernizing state, however he may subvert its tendencies toward totalism and psychism. We may therefore say that the Chinese Communists could find it feasible to demand that their intellectuals be "Red" *as well as* "expert"—but not *instead of.*

The Maoists realize this more than they admit. The August 1966 document issued by the Central Committee of the Party announcing policies of the Great Proletarian Cultural Revolution includes a special paragraph granting relative immunity to scientists and technicians. It specifies that those among them "who have made valuable contributions" should be "protected" and "assisted in gradually transforming their world outlook and styles of work." The operative words here are "protected" and "gradually."

Kurt Mendelssohn, an English physicist who visited China in September–October 1966, was in fact impressed with the technological and scientific progress there as compared with what he had found during a visit six years earlier.[11] He went on to describe a working style evolved by Chinese scientists for combining Redness and expertness, as illustrated by a paper published by a research group with the intriguing title "Research on the theory of elementary particles carried out under the brilliant illumination of Mao Tse-tung's thought." Dr. Mendelssohn points out that the paper was both serious and advanced in its intellectual content, but that successive steps in the reasoning process are "copiously underlined by reference to Mao's works." And a section of the paper dealing with the correlation of theory and experiment in studying internal structure of elementary particles bears the heading "How can you catch tiger cubs without entering the tiger's lair?"—a folk saying of the kind that Mao is fond of quoting.* Yet even if we assume this obeisance to Mao's

---

* Similar principles apply more generally in technology and construction. Crediting the thought of Mao Tse-tung with such achievements as large new factories, dams, and airports has not precluded the use of up-to-date methods and materials in building them. But once achieved, the technology itself is "proletarianized" by becoming the center of a new genre of expressive art. Blending dance, music, and lyrics from traditional folk songs and contemporary Maoist visions, artistic works have appeared with such titles as "Iron Man Wang" and "Three Power Lines Come to the Countryside." Another, "The Rising Sun," tells "the stirring story of how the family members of the workers of Taching oilfield, nurtured on the think-

thought to be no more than an accepted ritual, the scientists who employ it are likely to do so with a slight sense of absurdity. For they are well aware that their accomplishments depend not on Mao's works but on their own scientific knowledge. Or to put the matter another way, disciplined intellectual effort in these areas of work is incompatible with Maoist psychism.*

Evidence to this effect can be found in the questioning of dogma by scientists in Eastern Europe. One physicist in East Berlin, for instance, made the claim recently that the deterministic assumptions of Marxism-Leninism are untenable when viewed in the light of contemporary quantum mechanics, since the latter has refuted the general concept of absolute casuality.[13] Such a statement cannot be viewed as merely idiosyncratic; rather, it is an erudite rejection of totalism and psychism by a scientific intellectual with a particular bent for wider theoretical issues. And however the Cultural Revolution struggles against

---

ing of Mao Tse-tung, get organized to engage in collective productive labor and take the road of the revolution." Its six acts written, sung, and performed by those very workers and their families, it was reportedly presented 133 times before 220,000 Peking theatergoers, and "the success of the play of these ordinary working people was a resounding slap in the face of the bourgeois 'experts' and 'authorities.' " [12]

* One might claim that it could lead to a different kind of "psychism": the observation of some contemporary physicists that the more one probes into the structure of smaller and smaller particles, the less certain one is about the nature or even existence of physical matter. But here we are dealing with an observation *on* nature rather than a substitution of the psychic state of the observer *for* it, and we cannot apply the term psychism in the sense we have been using it.

this form of "impurity" of thought—or modern revisionism —it is bound to arise from within.

Maoist dilemmas around technology and psychism arise also in the Faustian realm of nuclear weapons.[14] These date back to the original announcement of America's dropping of an atomic bomb on Hiroshima on August 6, 1945. The Party's first more or less official reaction was a fairly conventional one, as suggested by the title of an article that appeared on August 9 in the *Liberation Daily*: "A Revolution in the Art of War." But just four days later Mao made an important speech in which he put the matter very differently:

> Can atom bombs decide wars? No, they can't. Atom bombs could not make Japan surrender. Without the struggles waged by the people, atom bombs by themselves would be of no avail. . . . Why didn't Japan surrender when the two bombs were dropped on her, and why did she surrender as soon as the Soviet Union sent troops? Some of our comrades, too, believe that the atom bomb is all-powerful; that is a big mistake. . . . What influence has made these comrades look upon the atom bomb as something miraculous? Bourgeois influence. . . . The theory that "weapons decide everything," the purely military viewpoint, a bureaucratic style of work divorced from the masses, individualist thinking and the like—all these are bourgeois influences in our ranks. We must constantly sweep these bourgeois things out of our ranks just as we sweep dust.

Without denying the validity of Mao's stress upon human factors in war, we may note two highly significant themes in the passage. The first is his insistent underestimation of the part played by the atomic bomb in bringing about Japan's surrender.* The second theme is Mao's highly revealing way of responding to this revolution in destructive technology: *Rather than tell his followers that the world itself has changed—or that man's relationship to death and life has altered—Mao instead exhorts them to renew their intrapsychic efforts at purification.* Without saying so directly, he leaves one with the impression that to explore the full implications of nuclear weapons as such would constitute another form of bourgeois impurity. Here are the beginnings of a nuclear psychism that has since emerged so prominently in Mao's thought.

Another example of the same tendency was his celebrated characterization of the bomb one year later as a "paper tiger." The metaphor was simultaneously applied to "reactionaries" in general, and since then has become one of the most popular as well as picturesque phrases in the Maoist lexicon—for "imperialism," "American imperialism," the Soviet Union, "revisionists," air power, and sea power. But one should nonetheless avoid the temptation to dismiss it as no more than a propagandistic rallying cry of a technologically backward country.

Mark Gayn, for instance, noted that when Mao used the

---

* Later evidence from Japanese sources has made it impossible to deny the enormous impact of the two atomic bombs upon the Japanese, even if one deplores their use and is convinced that the war could have been terminated not too much later without them. When he spoke, Mao could not have had access to any reliable information on what actually brought about Japan's surrender, but his immediate ideological reflex is to question the influence of nuclear weapons.

metaphor during a conversation with him in 1947, the Chairman added the comment that "we're too primitive to fear the atomic bomb." Gayn saw this as a combination of ignorance and insight:

> For if Mao knew little of the devastating effect of the A-bomb, and especially of radioactivity, he was also the first leader to detect, only a year after the tragedy in Hiroshima, the one striking flaw in nuclear power . . . [that] its effectiveness against primitive countries is limited—unless the user wanted to do the unthinkable and erase the target country with all its life off the map.[15]

Gayn is surely right about Mao's raising significant issues concerning military and especially political limitations of nuclear weapons, in contrast to the tendency of many leaders in other countries to embrace the weapons as all-powerful deities in a pattern I have elsewhere called "nuclearism." But the idea that primitive countries need not fear nuclear weapons is, at the very least, highly questionable, consistent in tone with other Maoist imagery even more clearly psychistic in nature. Thus, assertions have been made that Mao's doctrine on "people's war" is a "spiritual atomic bomb" possessed only by China which is much more powerful than actual nuclear weapons; and that the concept of nuclear weapons being decisive in warfare is put forth by modern revisionists to "frighten the revolutionary people into giving up resistance." We sense that Maoist psychism concerning nuclear weapons, as elsewhere, is intimately bound up with the fear of the death of the Chinese Revolution.

This tendency becomes more pronounced in Mao's claim, made during an exchange with Jawaharlal Nehru in

Moscow in 1957, that nuclear war would at worst kill half of mankind and "the other half would remain while imperialism would be razed to the ground and the whole world would become socialist; in a number of years there would be twenty-seven hundred million people again and definitely more." And we encounter its most extreme expression of all in a comment on atomic war that appeared in an unsigned 1960 editorial in *Red Flag*, the theoretical organ of the Party, which was believed either to have been written by Mao or directly inspired by him:

> Should the imperialists impose such sacrifices on the peoples of various countries, we believe that, just as the experience of the Russian Revolution and the Chinese Revolution shows, those sacrifices would be rewarded. On the debris of imperialism, the victorious people would create very swiftly a civilization thousands of times higher than the capitalist system and a truly beautiful future for themselves.[16]

One is left with the uneasy feeling that the author of this passage comes close to seeing nuclear holocaust as a vehicle for the realization of revolutionary immortality. The apocalyptic image of world-destruction at the hands of terrible nuclear deities, followed by a magnificent collective resurrection of true believers, joins Maoist psychism with a form of ardent nuclearism.

Mao's stress upon nuclear afterlife, upon the general capacity to survive nuclear war, sometimes resembles that of the early Herman Kahn (as expressed in his book *On Thermonuclear War*). Mao's musings on the subject, as recorded by Snow, reveal, first, a certain disdain for those who call attention to the power of the weapons:

Americans also said very much about the destructiveness of the atom bomb and Khrushchev had made a big noise about that. They had all surpassed him in this respect, so that he was more backward than they, was that not so?

Mao then becomes almost lyrical in his description of the persistence of life in the Bikini Islands six years after the nuclear tests there, referring to an American report he had read:

> When [the American investigators] first entered the island they had to cut open paths through the undergrowth. They found mice scampering about and fish swimming in the streams as usual. The well water was potable, plantation foliage was flourishing, and birds were twittering in the trees. Probably there had been two bad years after the tests, but nature had gone on. In the eyes of nature and the birds, the mice and the trees, the atom bomb was a paper tiger. Possibly man has less stamina than they? [17]

The ironic final question suggests that, after all, Mao lacks complete faith in man's capacity to survive nuclear weapons.* And the whole passage reflects on East Asian identification with eternal nature as a mode of symbolic immortality to an extent that the issue of *human* survival becomes almost irrelevant. But the overall tone is Mao's characteristic one of minimization of nuclear destruction.

We thus encounter in relationship to the weapons a convergence of psychism and nuclearism—the one a response of intrapsychic purification, the other an embrace of the

---

* One could also interpret the ironic question as suggesting that man has *more* stamina than trees, birds, and mice—though this interpretation seems less likely than the one I suggest above.

*new deity, both calling forth denial and psychic numbing
to fend off an accurate picture of potential nuclear killing.*

This convergence of psychism and nuclearism was in
some ways furthered by China's own acquisition of the
weapons. Not only did she bend all efforts toward obtaining them (unlike several other countries, such as Japan
and India, who despite possessing the capacity have held
back), but when successful in doing so greeted the new
possessions with joyous embrace and celebration of national power. Again these attitudes are hardly unknown
among other countries. But with the Chinese the achievement became associated with pride of autonomous accomplishment vis-à-vis both the Soviet Union (which had
withdrawn its nuclear assistance) and the United States
(which had repeatedly underestimated China's nuclear
capacity). In addition, the Chinese have ideologically
connected the weapons with their militant world view.
They speak of their "mastery" of them as having given
"great encouragement to the revolutionary peoples of the
world in their struggles" and having "boosted the mo-
rale" [18] of all revolutionaries. Such nuclearism reached a
climax with China's first successful hydrogen bomb test
explosion, which occurred at the height of the Cultural
Revolution in June 1967: the news was greeted with singing and dancing in the streets, the waving of little red
books of quotations from Mao, and pronouncements
everywhere on the source of the great achievement as the
invincible Thought of Mao Tse-tung.*

* The *Peking Review* of June 23, 1967, reports: "Peking was jubi-
lant when it got the news late in the night of June 17, and the
reception centre of the Party Central Committee and the State

But all this is by no means the entire story of China's—and Mao's—encounter with nuclear weapons. For instance, in November 1964, just one month after its first detonation of a nuclear weapon, the Chinese chastised Japan for her alliance with the United States and warned her of the danger of being "pushed into the abyss of nuclear calamity." The warning could be viewed as a political use of the newly acquired weapon and to a certain extent a form of nuclearism. But the phrase "abyss of nuclear calamity," which the Chinese have used frequently in other situations as well, reflects a recognition that precisely such a calamity stalks everyone—even "primitive" countries like China herself (if the possessor of nuclear weapons can still so view herself). It is true that the Chinese, even after their acquisition of the weapons, have continued to employ the paper tiger image—though inevitably about the other fellow's nuclear bombs rather than their own. The general historical experience, however, has been that the very possession of nuclear weapons in a vari-

---

Council was the focus of celebrating throngs. Carrying portraits of Chairman Mao, holding red banners high and waving their *Quotations from Chairman Mao Tse-tung*, people converged on the centre to offer congratulations. Cheers, gongs, drums and firecrackers resounded throughout the night. Congratulatory messages unanimously described the successful explosion of China's first hydrogen bomb as marking the start of a new stage in the development of nuclear weapons in China, as an event proclaiming the total bankruptcy of the nuclear monopoly blackmail practised by the U. S. imperialists and the Soviet revisionists and a demonstration that for the Chinese people armed with the brilliant thought of Mao Tse-tung, there is no height that cannot be scaled, no fortress that cannot be stormed and no force that can hold back their victorious advance."

ety of ways forces upon a nation some recognition of the actualities of their destructive power, and China is no exception.*

Indeed the Maoists have never entirely repudiated that initial recognition of nuclear weapons as constituting a "revolution in the art of war." This recognition has been reflected in China's international political and military stance—a stance characterized by what one commentator has called "prudent aggressiveness," [20] and another the tendency to "bluster belligerently while behaving with extreme caution." [21] This behavior is consistent with a side of Mao's thought we have insufficiently emphasized, his own pragmatism in certain areas, especially that of coping with one's enemies: "Strategically we should despise all our enemies, but tactically we should take them all seriously . . . despise the enemy with respect to the whole, but

---

* Chinese views on the spread of nuclear weapons suggest such a recognition. Prior to their own initial detonation of 1964, the Chinese tended to stress the advantages of nuclear proliferation, especially (but not exclusively) to communist countries, as a means of breaking the nuclear monopoly of America and the Soviet Union (the French decision for nuclear development was looked upon approvingly), and of furthering the cause of peace. But since that time, Chinese attitudes toward proliferation have been more muted and rather ambivalent. Nor have the Chinese demonstrated any inclination toward nuclear sharing. Moreover, they have in various ways shown awareness of the limitations of their nuclear capacity and the dangers to them posed by America's superior nuclear weapons and by the widely publicized inclinations of certain American militarists toward destroying the main Chinese nuclear installations. The Chinese have also reiterated their program for universal nuclear disarmament, declared that China would under no circumstances be the first to use nuclear weapons, and invited other nuclear powers to join them in a "no first use" agreement.[19]

. . . take him seriously with respect to each and every concrete question." We may thus say that in matters of destructive potential, and especially nuclear weapons, technology impinges constantly upon psychism and renders it more and more untenable. But nuclearism in other quarters—the United States, Russia, France, and (aspiringly) the rest of the world—also reverberates upon the special Maoist combination of psychism, nuclearism, and pragmatism.

A closely related confrontation concerns the technology of population control. Best estimates of China's present population usually range from seven hundred to eight hundred million, with the anticipation, at the current growth rate, of one billion people by about 1985.[22] We have observed Maoist China's proud sense of her own vast numbers—her frequent reminders that more than one-fourth of mankind is Chinese—to be an assertion of immortal cultural substance, as linked with the communist revolution. Also contributing to a general disinclination toward population control are such divergent influences as the old Confucian stress upon large families and upon the absolute filial obligation to produce posterity;* intense nationalism; and a purist Marxist position (no longer held to in other Marxist countries), which bitterly condemns any suggestion that Malthusian dangers of overpopulation might apply to a communist society with "rational" control over production and distribution. So strongly have the

* Mencius, Confucius' great disciple, said: "There are three unfilial acts, and the lack of posterity is the greatest."

Maoists felt on the subject that an editorial in the *People's Daily* in April 1952 went so far as to describe birth control as "a means of killing Chinese without shedding blood."

But given the relentless realities of feeding and housing the ever increasing number of Chinese, this purist attitude could simply not be sustained. And during the last half of the 1950s, especially during the liberal period of the "Hundred Flowers" (1956–1957), the idea of birth control began to take hold as a respectable ideological position. To be sure, that position had to be specifically disassociated from "reactionary Malthusian doctrine." China was adopting birth-control measures (as Premier Chou En-lai put it) "to protect women and children and bring up and educate our younger generation in a way conducive to the health and prosperity of the nation." But the outcome in any case was an energetic national program that included the building of factories for the manufacture of contraceptives, widespread mass-media dissemination of information about family planning, and the spread of birth-control clinics and information centers from the cities into the rural areas.

But this pragmatic (and humane) interlude ended abruptly in 1958 because, as we might well suspect, it was incompatible with the heroic visions of the Great Leap Forward. Indeed at that time Maoist spokesmen took the extraordinary position that China was not overpopulated at all, that in respect to the vast demands of socialist reconstruction she was "underpopulated" and in need of more manpower. The President of Peking University, Ma Yin-ch'u, who had earlier emphasized the hardships of uncontrolled population growth for the Chinese people, now suddenly found himself denounced as a "rightist" and a "Malthusian," and was subsequently dismissed from his university post. Inevitably, the psychism pervading the Great Leap entered into the highly symbolic issue of population control: *reasoned technical planning for the feeding and housing of China's masses gave way to a psychological insistence upon their mystical strength and invincibility.* For at that moment in particular China's immortal substance could not be questioned; birth control became an assault upon Chinese power, an attack upon revolutionary immortality.

Yet during the period of liberalization following the Great Leap, especially in 1962, birth-control partisans again spoke out. Once more attempts were made to limit population—with encouragement of late marriage and small families—and these policies continue to the present. But the effort has been somewhat sluggish and, in the opinion of knowledgeable observers, very far indeed from coping with China's actual situation. Moreover, one suspects that it has been especially slack during the Cultural Revolution.

Of the greatest importance, however, is the fact that the Cultural Revolution does *not* appear to be making a major point of *undermining* efforts at birth control. This at least suggests a limitation to its psychism in one of the most fundamental of all areas. For no regime ruling China can avoid being impressed by material evidence of population increase and its consequences, however it seeks to shield itself from such evidence. The technology of population control, therefore, could in the long run be one of the most significant restraints upon Maoist psychism and totalism.

We sense in Mao, as in Chinese policy in general, a profound inner division concerning technology. As a twentieth-century man and a great revolutionary leader he is profoundly drawn to it, knowing it to be essential both to his revolution and to the welfare of his people. Yet his resentment of technology seems equally profound, as revealed in the heroic desperation he brings to his efforts to replace it with psychic power and with Chinese "essence." Observing his dilemma, we in the West can ill afford to gloat, living as we do in societies being devoured by their own technologies. We know that Mao is hardly the first to discover—or to cause his most devoted disciples to discover—that one cannot have it both ways.

VIII

TIME AND TOTALISM: PSYCHOLOGICAL LIMITATIONS

MAN'S PSYCHIC state can be pushed just so far. Or, when pushed to extremes, these can be maintained for just so long. Then psychological and historical forces converge to place limits upon individual psychism and group totalism. In my study of Chinese thought reform I suggested three such limitations: mounting response of inner antagonism or "hostility of suffocation"; the effective penetration of the "idea-tight milieu control" by outside influences that undermine the closed communication system; and a "law of diminishing conversions" operating among those subjected to repeated reform experiences, according to which inner enthusiasm is increasingly replaced by outward compliance.[1] I would suggest that all three patterns have been prominent in limiting the totalism and psychism of the Cultural Revolution.

There can be little doubt of the widespread experience of hostility of suffocation. The evidence comes to us not only from observations of visitors and defectors, but from the Chinese press and radio, and especially from the great-character posters so prominent throughout. The tones of anger and hatred in the accusations and counter-accusations reported by all of these sources have been startling even to those familiar with the explosive series of mass campaigns carried out by the Communist regime since its inception in 1949. As in the case of these earlier campaigns much of the initial anger associated with the Cultural Revolution was part of a command performance. But very quickly there emerged hatreds of a more unfocused nature—including the rage of people pressed beyond balance and pushed into untenable stances of psychism. This rage was expressed in the violent acts of Mao's opponents, and occasionally in those of their words that broke through the Maoist control of the communications media. And it was also expressed in the vitriolic language of Mao's supporters. For when hostility of suffocation begins to suffuse a national atmosphere, anger takes hold as a prevailing if unstable idiom of discourse, irrespective of who is shouting and who is being shouted at. *

An additional manifestation of the hostility of suffocation goes beyond hostility itself—withdrawing from the overall psychic and physical struggle. We are finally hearing of groups of alienated Chinese youth, a phenomenon that must have been present, or at least latent, for some time. They go by the evocative name of "wanderers," and a description of them appearing in a Shanghai newspaper in July 1967 makes them sound familiar indeed:

* Contributing to the hostility of suffocation is the classical populist dilemma: the masses are idealized as the source of virtue and wisdom, but ultimately led and manipulated by an elite group of organizers who are committed to the populist doctrine. Compounding the problem is the very great difficulty (experienced by officials throughout the world) of coping with contemporary problems of historical change and successfully managing any large-scale society.

In the course of the great Cultural Revolution a number of people have emerged who do not pay attention to
state affairs and who stay out of the revolutionary movement. These people are called wanderers. They take an
attitude of non-intervention in the struggle between the
proletariat and the bourgeoisie. Instead of fighting on the
battlefront, they wander about school campuses, parks
and streets; they spend their time in swimming pools and
playing chess and cards. . . . Whenever they are required to reveal an attitude, they just issue vague statements. They have voluntarily withdrawn from the political stage.[2]

The familiarity becomes even more striking when the article goes on to claim that these wanderers have "lost their
bearings" even though they may appear to be "blissful."
The temptation to bestow upon the group the name "Chinese hippies" should probably have been resisted, pending
a bit more information about them and especially about
their inner lives. But that characterization was immediately made by at least one Western commentator. We are
probably justified in saying that, like hippies, wanderers
are in some degree explorers of the self, although we have
no reason to believe that they necessarily embrace the full
range of hippie patterns.* For this they must inevitably be
denounced as people who "put self-interest above all else."

---

* Among hippie patterns I include a form of nonviolent rejection of
and withdrawal from ordinary participation in society, a stress upon
experiential intensity (including use of drugs), and a variety of
explorations in individual and group intimacy—all resulting in the
formation of a rather discrete subculture with its own language and
mores.

If contemporary Chinese wanderers are not quite hippies, however, they do seem to be related to resistive, innovative, and in various ways "alienated" youth groups throughout the world. Like these other youth groups, they reflect large confusions accompanying rapid historical change and the search for alternatives to existing social identities. And it is also possible to find historical antecedents to them in the Taoists of traditional China who sought escape from the demanding Confucian social order by way of withdrawal and mysticism. But whatever their historical and cultural roots, the wanderers' emergence has undoubtedly been greatly intensified by the Cultural Revolution itself. The same newspaper article thus includes among their number

> some people who have made mistakes in the course of the Cultural Revolution movement; others who took part in it for personal reasons fearing it would turn against them but who tried to stop half-way when they realized their goal could not be realized; others who were so-called "veteran rebels" who after a long period became tired of the civil wars among the mass organizations to which they belonged, and instead of seeking ways to stop the civil wars and making efforts to fight the common enemy, flew the flag of truce to avoid trouble.

In other words, people who felt hemmed in and fearful, who chose withdrawal from, rather than direct resistance to, what they must have come to view as absurd physical and verbal struggles around them.

Such people are the very antithesis of the official version of the ideal youth, totally and unquestioningly committed to Maoist views and policies. Wanderers, it would seem, care little for Mao's thoughts or visions, and after giving lip service to them, seek either their own pleasure or a bit of quietude. But the article about them warns that although they look "passive about the Revolution now," in the future "they will become bitter and tough and no longer peaceful"—possibly a projection of Maoists' own violent feelings, but perhaps also to some extent an accurate perception of the hostility of suffocation underneath the wanderers' apparent passivity. Moreover, by causing all schools to be closed for more than a year and encouraging the Red Guards to travel about the country and participate in various "movements" on behalf of Maoist aims, the Cultural Revolution could be said to have made additional contributions to a style of psychic and physical "wandering."

Concerning the second psychological limitation, the undermining of milieu control by ideas from the outside, we may again point to the specter of modern revisionism. There is one aspect of this specter around which Maoists have undoubtedly been able to mobilize considerable fear and antagonism: Chinese resentment and injured pride over Russian attitudes perceived as patronizing in regard to "helping" a junior communist partner, over what I spoke of before as a situation of counterfeit nurturance. And there have been very real bases for antagonism between the two countries concerning ideological and tactical matters. Yet it seems clear that Chinese minds have been indelibly marked by "revisionist" images—especially by images of liberalization and pragmatism as alternatives to totalism and psychism.

Concrete evidence of this has been the appearance in

China of a "New Trend," [3] apparently influenced by revisionist as well as by independent Marxist principles, and possibly by egalitarian non-Marxist ones as well. Whether the New Trend is an actual organization or a loose body of thought is not clear, but there are indications that it raises fundamental questions about the uses of power by both Maoist and anti-Maoist groups during and prior to the Cultural Revolution. Human history can be defined as the continuous spread of ideas and images from mind to mind and group to group, and in our present electronic age it becomes particularly futile to attempt to seal off any collectivity from impinging outside currents. China's extremely advanced human control mechanisms, vast geographical terrain, and relatively limited communications technology would seem to make her an ideal nation for such sealing-off. But these Chinese attributes can in fact do no more than slow down the mental invasion, and in the Cultural Revolution they have served mainly to feed a double illusion—that of milieu control itself, and that of the capacity of a milieu, once penetrated, to cast off the outside evil and re-establish its internal purity.

The third limitation on psychism and totalism, the "law of diminishing conversions," follows directly upon the other two. Here we encounter the built-in contradiction of psychism: in its zeal to replace technology with mind, it tends to interfere with precisely the internal work necessary to accomplish real individual conversion and general social transformation. While extolling the mind and the will as creators of external reality, the Cultural Revolution has lacked the patient assurance and steady effort necessary for genuine reshaping (or realignment) of mental processes.* This assurance and effort could be said to have been present during earlier thought reform campaigns, though even then results tended to be mixed. The Cultural Revolution utilized such standard thought reform elements as criticism and self-criticism, group-mediated shame and guilt, and the by now classic Maoist subject matter. But public demonstration was substituted for internal experience, activism for psychic work, violence for persuasion—and ultimately, one suspects, uneasy obedience for significant inner change.

We see now the full paradox of psychism: there is the insistent substitution of the psychic state for the machine; but the psychic work required for authentic inner change is in turn replaced by an *image* of the change having already taken place. So predominant does the vision of revolutionary immortality become that confusion exists not only between mind and thing but between mentation and external action.

Confronted by these psychological limitations, Mao begins to manifest what has been called the "end of charisma"—the loss of some of the magnetic hold he has had upon his followers.[4] For that charismatic hold, I would suggest, depends upon the leader's capacity to convey to his followers a convincing mode of immortality, suffi-

* To be sure, the task itself—the kind of reshaping undertaken—was an impossible one, as I have tried to demonstrate. But in addition, and partly as a consequence, human manipulations during the Cultural Revolution were often performed in erratic and unsteady fashion.

ciently rewarding to enable them to weather the strain his demands may place upon their psychic capacities. In Mao's case the revolutionary mode offered has surely seemed increasingly imperfect to large numbers of former followers, and the more they have questioned it, the more he has asked of them. The result has been a vicious circle of the leader's strong demands, followers' mistrust and resentment, and escalated demands—the whole process intensified by the general anticipation of the leader's death.

This is part of the leader's loss of potency we spoke of before. He cannot totally avoid (in St. Mark's words) "Knowing in himself that virtue had gone out of him," but he seeks to fight off and compensate for such "knowledge." Followers may become even more quickly aware of his loss of the combination of "virtue" (purity) and power that they had originally responded to, and they in turn feel "lost" and pressed in unnatural and unfathomable directions. The negative side of their dependency and discipleship can then emerge: old resentments become newly reinforced. Principles of belief and guidelines for action, crystal clear until a moment ago, now become hazy and obscure. Assuming all this to have been the experience of many of Mao's followers, they are left with the alternative of either allying themselves with the opposition, withdrawing and becoming "wanderers," pretending to remain good Maoists while feeling themselves less and less enthusiastic, or becoming all the more zealous as a means of denying their doubts and suppressing their anger. But the possibility of undergoing a profound and sustained conversion to Maoist doctrine, as held forth as an ideal of the Cultural Revolution, becomes increasingly remote.

Can we understand these psychological limitations as social expressions of what Freud called the "reality principle"? If so, what is the "reality" involved? It would seem to have something to do with the very "human nature" the Maoists have tried to deny. I do not mean human nature as a rigidly set entity but as a general psychobiological potential within a particular (though always changing) cultural and historical matrix. Human nature thus understood is highly flexible, yet at the same time an imposer of limits. One of these limits is the need for a certain amount of harmony between the evidence of the senses and socially shared images of self and world.

From this standpoint one may view Russian revisionism and de-Stalinization as historical and psychological inclinations toward the harmonies of human nature and away from the excesses of totalism and psychism. Mao might have been expected to welcome these tendencies, having been so long in conflict with Stalin over the latter's policies toward the Chinese Revolution—policies Mao thought to be out of touch with the actualities of the Chinese environment. But his vision of Chinese revolutionary immortality took precedence over all other influences; the contaminations of modern revisionism had to be attacked. In a very important sense the entire constellation of the Great Leap Forward and Cultural Revolution was called forth to prove the falseness of the idea of human nature as one such contamination, and then to demonstrate the superior psychic *and technological* possibilities of home-grown revolutionary purity as the shortest and truest path to that ultimate destination of Marxist history—the "stage of communism." But both movements turned out instead to be vivid demonstrations of the psychological limitations of the Maoist vision. The false statistics of the Great Leap epitomized this limitation. These falsities are a classic example of the totalistic tendency to view ideological assumptions as "truer than truth," and they may well come to be viewed as an equally classic expression of the undermining of psychism through the convergence of technology and "human nature." *

Under such conditions much of man's imagery about his world goes out of joint, notably his images of time. In the same poem in which Mao recalled how "we dared command the sun and moon to bring a new day," there is also the phrase "I curse the flux of time." The leader's efforts to recall the heroic past become associated with the unyielding nostalgia of an old man who has known better days and is ill equipped to cope with new situations. I have in other contexts described this pattern as the "mode of restoration," the urge to return to a mythological past in order to draw upon its ennobling symbols for present sustenance and future direction.[5] For Mao the revolutionary past is pure, while the present—tainted as it is by "modern revisionism" and by a technology that insists on being more than an extension of spirit or will—is profoundly im-

---

* Here and elsewhere in the essay I have stressed the interplay of the psychological and historical to the neglect of questions of social structure. An alternative analysis could emphasize the Maoist attack upon consolidating social institutions of all kinds (as epitomized by Russian revisionism), and an attempt to create new institutions that lend themselves to continuous revolutionary ferment. But I believe that the psychohistorical limitations I emphasize are consistent with such an analysis, and in fact underlie the "structural" difficulties Maoists have encountered.

pure. But the restorationist tends to be deeply (though unconsciously) attracted to the very symbols of contemporary evil he so passionately condemns. And one must at least raise the possibility that the extravagant tone of the Cultural Revolution can be partly explained by a hidden attraction *felt by Mao and the Maoists* toward the entire revisionist world view—including its accommodation both to technology and human nature. To the extent that this paradox prevails, it exerts a further limitation upon the entire movement because it requires Maoists to struggle against these tendencies, not only as put forth by their "enemies" but as exerting seductive appeal within themselves.

At the same time we know the Cultural Revolution to have embraced a seemingly opposite and perhaps even more intense "mode of transformation"—a demand for almost instant remaking of society and man, according to the model of the thought of Mao. This wavering between restorationism and transformationism is not unique, given the related psychological nature of the two polar modes. What is unique is the extremity of each: the restorationist "curse" of the "flux of time," and need to create a revolution on the old model for young Chinese who "had never fought a war and never seen an imperialist or known capitalism and power"; and the transformationist insistence that the rate of change be ever accelerated, that man and society change overnight.

What results is a pattern of conflicting demands, which we may term *nostalgic preoccupation with newness*. And the pattern is especially confusing to those who responded most enthusiastically to the original call. For instance, groups of Red Guards who had originally been hailed as young heroes, as the purest of the pure, were being denounced just a few months later (when felt to be too slow to coordinate their activities with other groups) as "old rebels," as "lonely fighters" who "live in a tiny little circle" and "lie on the couch of their great deeds." Originally praised for their militancy in "breaking down the old and establishing the new," they were denounced for irresponsible "showing of muscles" and "participation in riotous events." So quick were shifts in prescribed standards of behavior that even the most loyal Maoist could no longer be sure of the proper "Way." Not infrequently the Red Guards themselves, the very agents of rebirth, loomed as the main threat to efficient Maoist control. Confusion in relationship to past and future—to time itself—had created a psychic flux so extreme that yesterday's command became today's crime.

With standards changing so quickly, months passed during which virtually no social forms could be described as stable—a good definition of chaos. Attacks upon "those in authority" extended diffusely to virtually all government leaders; violent clashes took place between contending groups within the Red Guards and Revolutionary Rebels; there was massive shifting of sides amidst a sea of ideological fervor and opportunism; and considerable breakdown in work schedules, transportation, and communications throughout various parts of the country. It became difficult indeed for anyone to be certain as to which group was furthering revolutionary immortality.

Although rarely asked in public, one suspects that during 1966 and 1967 life in China frequently became

dominated by the question *"Where does purity lie?"*
Should one or should one not destroy a bust of Sun Yat-sen,
an early revolutionary to be sure but a non-communist
one, and replace it with a bust of Mao Tse-tung? How
should one distinguish between genuine and counterfeit
Red Guards? If the Shanghai Commune was to be an ideal
model for all of China, what was one to think of the Triple
Alliance (revolutionary organizations, Army, and pro-
Maoist cadres) which replaced it just a few days after it
came into being? Granted that "demolition bombs and
hand grenades will be thrown," who was to throw them
and at which targets? Under such conditions of chaotic
flux one ran out of both reliable friends and reliable enemies. The path to revolutionary immortality became ob-
scured and enduring emotional commitment to it or anything else became close to impossible.

Related to this exaggerated flux was the transformationist myth of eliminating the non-revolutionary past. Here
the Cultural Revolution met another impasse: nothing in
the past can be entirely eliminated, nothing is entirely lost
to history. There was a rather touching illustration of this
principle during the pre-Cultural Revolution attack upon
humanism in 1964, in the experience of a writer and literary theorist named Shao Ch'uan-lin.[6] Although himself
formerly a severe critic of revisionism, Shao objected to
the narrowness of the anti-revisionist campaign and to its
demand for oversimplified portrayal of literary subjects.
He was then accused of embracing "bourgeois humanism"
and "bourgeois realism," and he and his supporters were
labeled "potential or real fellow travelers of the revisionists." But he defended his literary vision as one in which

he wished "to see largeness from smallness, and a world in a grain of *rice*" (emphasis added). This in turn, however, led his critics to associate him with a previous literary "bad example," Hu Feng, who in 1955 had been arrested for counter-revolutionary activities, and had similarly spoken of the importance of "ordinary things" and of finding "a world in a grain of *sand*" (emphasis added). These critics did not go further and identify the actual origin of the expression in a poem of William Blake. Yet in that origin perhaps lies the real significance of the episode: the historical transmission and ultimate survival not only of the phrase itself but of the vision it suggests. For in Blake's original lines—"To see a World in a Grain of Sand/And a Heaven in a Wild Flower,/Hold Infinity in the palm of your hand/And eternity in an hour"—we encounter powerful alternatives to revolutionary immortality, suggestions of experiential transcendence and embrace of nature which have long been called forth by mystics and poets. To his perpetual need for *some* form of symbolic immortality man brings a combination of past historical experience and fresh imagination, neither of which can be fully eliminated by totalistic programs. There is always the possibility of the emergence of a mode other than that prescribed.

Maoists have had more specific difficulties with the historical record. We have observed the surfacing during the Cultural Revolution of past failures and conflicts, especially those in relationship to the Great Leap Forward. And we have spoken of the related problem of negative reinterpretation of revolutionary accomplishments of distinguished leaders-turned-evil-opponents—the devaluing of Liu Shao-chi's "How To Be a Good Communist" in the eyes of the generation or two of cadres whose moral perspectives had been importantly shaped by it. Also in connection with dishonoring Liu, the Cultural Revolution has struggled with a specific historical event: the 1936 "confessions" of a group of revolutionaries renouncing communist beliefs—apparently made on direct orders from the Party hierarchy, then represented by Liu—in order to effect their release from Kuomintang prisons. The Maoist attack upon both Liu and those who had made the confessions (most had risen under Liu's patronage to become high functionaries) took an indirect form in which the principle of negative historical reinterpretation was carried still further. It focused upon another "revolutionary," who also made a prominent "confession," Li Hsiu-Ch'eng, a leader of the Taiping Rebellion of 1848–1865. When a leading historian recently presented new evidence suggesting that this confession too had been a conscious form of deception and that Li had remained true to his principles, the historian was publicly denounced and his findings dismissed as contrary to the teaching of Chairman Mao. During the course of the Cultural Revolution the scholarly journal that had originally published the article was also denounced. There were hints connecting the two historical episodes, and a Maoist principle concerning the general study of history was reiterated: "The evaluation of a historical figure is not judgment on a dead man but the drawing of a line between revolutionaries and counter-revolutionaries." [7]

In the above sequence we can observe a longstanding Chinese cultural tendency to focus concretely upon manipulative reinterpretations of historical events as moral models for the present. In the extreme Maoist version of this tendency (as Kahn and Feuerwerker[8] explain), "the historian moves from the classroom to the platform . . . historiography moves from an effort to discover what actually was [Ranke's hope] to an effort to confirm what in fact should be. The past, that is, serves the present not by illuminating it but by defining it, by justifying it." But the problem is that "the historian must . . . [be] guided only by the Maoist star that signals . . . while the shifting clouds of domestic and international policy cast doubts as to the direction from which the beacon really beckons." During the Cultural Revolution the historical beacon has at times seemed to beckon simultaneously from several conflicting directions. And given the acceleration of history—in our times in general and in China in particular—falsifications and strained reinterpretations, together with the human pressures these bring about, catch up more quickly with their perpetrators than they did in the past.

This ineradicable historical legacy brings us back once more to those vague but persistent concepts of "humanism," "human feelings," and "human nature," derived as these are from a wide spectrum of Eastern and Western cultural traditions. They are particularly powerful concepts because they are both biologically rooted and actively intertwined with the ongoing historical process. The images and values they suggest—especially that of a nurturing concern for human life itself—evolve from centuries of molding of man's innate psychic potential. In the process the terms themselves have become evocative symbols around which political and ethical movements have long rallied. Separately and in combination, Western "humanism," Eastern "human feelings," and universal "human nature" have come to suggest important expressions of the biosocial and creative modes of immortality. Nor can man, once having established these images, totally dissociate himself from them.

One can even say that every expression of resistance to the excesses of the Cultural Revolution involves a reassertion of some such alternative to the prevailing blueprint for revolutionary immortality. Individual and group jealousies among leaders, rivalries between Red Guard units, mutual hostilities between Maoists on the one hand and "class enemies" and "those in authority" on the other—all of these are associated with alternative assumptions about the way life could or should be, on the basis of prior images of human continuity. Such alternative images are part of every individual life, at least during our century, and because of them man can never be viewed as totally manipulable.

Suppressed modes of immortality, moreover, can re-emerge suddenly and unexpectedly. This was illustrated by a rather homey incident reported in the Chinese press about a woman whose husband, a Party cadre, had been accused during the Cultural Revolution of being a counterrevolutionary. The wife "grumbled" and told her husband: "You have always worked for the community and neglected the family. We have had a hard time for more than ten years. Now you have become a counter-revolutionary!" What she meant was that she had relinquished her stress upon family (or upon biological immortality) in favor of the regime (revolutionary immortality), but that this latter mode had suddenly been rendered meaningless by his public disgrace and she now must revert (one suspects) to the former one.

There is also a converse but analogous principle: the psychic consequences of toning down a totalist vision of revolutionary immortality. Such abrupt "desymbolization" and severance from a sense of continuous life can give rise to resentful disillusionment, feelings of emptiness, and a variety of conflicts. These feelings and conflicts are likely to be strongest in those who originally responded most zealously, notably the young. And we may assume that such reactions have had much to do with repeated difficulties reported in controlling the Red Guards, in getting them to go home, return to school, and resume normal lives. These difficulties cannot simply be attributed to the restlessness of young people who have tasted the pleasures of travel and political excitement. What these young people have "tasted" has been an intimation of immortality, only to find themselves suddenly cast out from that exultant state. One may go further and say that not only Red Guards but Maoist leaders, and even perhaps Mao himself, all face rebound psychological consequences of such undermining of the immortalizing mode to which they have committed themselves so totally. This in turn means facing the universal problems from which they had been temporarily shielded by the power and purity of their revolutionary image—problems of human suffering, meaninglessness, and death itself.

All we have been saying suggests that psychism is limited by the nature of the mind, the body, and the world. While the three are aspects of a metaphysical whole, they cannot be substituted for one another, not even in the name of a transcendent revolutionary vision.

IX

BEYOND
THE LAST STAND

EVERYTHING about the Cultural Revolution renders one humble indeed at the very thought of prediction. I refer not only to the surprise with which it burst upon the world or even to its continuing unpredictability, so much as to its strange combination of futuristic tone and aura of the past. What we may say is that in many significant ways the Cultural Revolution has been a Last Stand.

① It is, as we have seen, the last stand of a great revolutionary against internal and external forces pressing him along that treacherous path from hero to despot. It is similarly the last stand of a collective expression ② of early revolutionary glory which he has epitomized. ③ And it is perceived on several symbolic levels as a last stand against death itself—of the leader, the revolution, and individual man in general.

But it can also be seen as a last stand of another less recognized entity—one we may call "militant rectitude"— a state of politicized straight-and-narrow moral earnestness pursued with unrelenting passion. Militant rectitude is an existential style that seems oddly old-fashioned during the latter part of our diffusely absurd twentieth century. Its model is the Chinese version of the "new revolutionary man," but we readily recognize Confucian and Christian, as well as communist contributions. During the Cultural Revolution (or at least its early phases) its exemplar was the totally mobilized, self-negating Red Guard, unswervingly dedicated to living out the immortalizing vision. What threatens militant rectitude is a very different kind of contemporary being I speak of as "protean man." [1] His psychological style, in direct contrast, is one of interminable exploration and flux, his self-process characterized by relatively easy shifts in belief and identification. He can readily embrace a set of convictions or respond to various kinds of symbols and images; his difficulty is maintaining inner connection with these for more than a brief experimental interlude. He is the very antithesis of Maoist militant rectitude in another aspect as well: his profound inner sense of absurdity, as given prominent expression in a prevailing tone of mockery. His mockery in fact is a specific rejection of moral earnestness and rectitude, a means of giving voice to the absence of "fit" between inner and outer worlds so characteristic of our era. It is *his* way of confronting death—and the contemporary disjointedness of life and death—rather than resorting to the Maoist's political-ideological quest for revolutionary immortality. Protean man in fact represents a generally post-Freudian, post-modern style almost totally absent from the image put forth by Maoists for the Chinese younger generation, but a style, I would suggest, that neither the Chinese nor anyone else will be completely able to resist.

There is a good deal of evidence that protean man is already emerging everywhere as an important psychological type—in the West, in Russia, in Japan (as I found in my research there), and (in a preliminary way) in other parts of East Asia. In fact, I encountered protean patterns in refugee intellectuals from the Chinese mainland, most of them young, whom I interviewed in depth in 1954 and 1955, suggesting that it has been at least latent in China for some time even if covered over by Maoist images of purity and rectitude. Nor is this surprising, since the protean style results from a radical breakdown in man's more structured relationship to traditional symbols— from psycho-historical dislocation—which China has over recent decades experienced in the extreme. It is also influenced by the world-wide revolution in mass communications which tends to flood the individual psyche with endlessly variable images in every sphere of life. This is one revolution that is only at an early stage in China, but it is certainly having its effect. The "wanderers" and advocates of the "New Trend" we spoke of before appear to be Chinese expressions of this protean process—of a more urban-cosmopolitan, experimental, and open life-style. Indeed, only the boldest kind of ideologues from the "old school" of revolutionary purity could have had the temerity to assume that in our present desymbolized nuclear universe an inclination toward the experimental and the absurd could be totally resisted.

Does all this suggest the likelihood of a pragmatic turn in China? One must always be cautious about drawing short-term political conclusions from general psychological observations. But such a turn would be consistent with the technological and psychological limitations to Maoist psychism we have discussed, as well as with the evolution of protean man. The fact is that the turn toward pragmatism has already begun.

From the early fall of 1967 the tone of official pronouncements began to alter. There has been an increasing emphasis (as personified by the influence of Chou En-lai) upon calls for restraint, for ending disorder, and for reestablishing stability and maximum production. The National Day (October 1) celebration marked a spirit of compromise—between individuals and groups (antagonists of the Cultural Revolution together on the reviewing stand), and in slogans employed (for instance, Lin Piao's face-saving but essentially moderate phrase, "Fight selfishness, criticize revisionism"). An important part of the trend has been a strong emphasis upon the reopening of all schools, though under the promised program of educational reform which lays great stress upon political (Maoist) thought and upon practical application of learning. The overall policy of compromise is represented as "the most recent instruction of Chairman Mao" and is accompanied by a vision of the entire nation becoming "the great school of the thought of Mao Tse-tung." A program of pragmatic retreat is thus described in the language of victory; a pause (or halt) in the extreme pursuit of revolutionary immortality is represented as its attainment.

In accordance with this trend the targets of criticism are no longer "those in authority" but *incorrigible* men in authority"—or, of even greater significance, "infantile leftists"—a Leninist image, which in this context means those who remain too intense in their Maoist militancy. The new political form is that of the "Revolutionary Committee," a somewhat muted successor to the Triple Alliance. There remains considerable evidence of discontent and conflict —reports in the Chinese press of groups having to be severely chastised for saying such things as "The military has seized political power," or for speaking of "the great alliance of fake revolutionaries." These are of course resentful expressions of disillusionment, and they contain sufficient truth to grate upon raw Maoist nerves. And as of the beginning of 1968 travelers coming from China continue to report outbreaks of violence and military intervention. But by and large the new stress is upon persuasion and reform, and even the Revolutionary Committee is spoken of as a "temporary authority"—with the implication that the plan is to return to more stable institutions, probably more like those which existed prior to the Cultural Revolution than during its most extreme phases.

Aiding this moderating trend are pockets of Chinese society that maintained an effective pragmatic approach throughout: the scientific and technical environments mentioned earlier, and various other relatively stable social, economic, and military arrangements. China will certainly not emerge unchanged by the Cultural Revolution, and the pragmatic turn will not be identical with the Russian model. It will surely retain many Maoist features (one must again keep in mind Mao's own pragmatic side), and it will probably continue to evolve in specifically Chinese directions. Nor can one say that similar campaigns against the death of the Revolution will not take place in the future—whether under the umbrella of renewed Cultural Revolution or under another name. But considering such factors as Mao's advanced age and his centrality to such a process, the general impediments to sustaining militant rectitude at this stage of world history, and the psychic and material cost to China of the events of 1966 and 1967, it is unlikely that anything approaching the excesses of the Cultural Revolution will soon be repeated.

Should one, then, as many have, speak of "the end of a dynasty"? The concept has special significance for China, conveying as it does a traditional image of dissolution of both power and virtue—of the Mandate of Heaven passing from the old group to the new. It suggests the shifting of immortal status and immortalizing capacity from one "family" to another, from one succession of anointed leaders to another. Yet the phrase may be only half-applicable. Mao's life has been so heroic and his ruling power so formidable that their impending termination does have some of the quality of an end of a dynasty—and even if Mao remains an active leader for a considerable period of time, one doubts that he will again have the authority to impose upon his country so extreme a revolutionary vision. But it may be more accurate to speak of the end of one "emperor's" rule, while the "dynasty" of Chinese Communism continues. One cannot predict future attitudes of Chinese leaders toward the Maoist image, but there is good reason to believe that for some time at least they will continue to hold the image on high even as they retreat from its excesses. The Mandate of Heaven may be passed not so much to a rival family as to one of a group of contending family members. And in this sense the Cultural Revolution can be viewed as a problem of individual and ideological succession, the resolution of which will require continuity rather than overthrow.

But any evaluation of these matters depends upon one's sense of the viability of the Chinese Communist regime,[2] and of what may be called "Chinese Communist culture." Some knowledgeable observers take a highly pessimistic view of China's future. They stress ways in which the Cultural Revolution has cut her off from her own past as well as from the rest of the contemporary world; how it has violated the young, both in the depth of disillusionment created in them and in the radical interruption of their educational process for periods of from one to two years; how it has undermined the main sources of the regime's authority and ruling capacity, the Party and the experienced bureaucracy; and how in various ways it has abused the shame sanction so central to the functioning of Chinese culture. But while one must recognize enormously destructive influences in precisely these areas, one must also consider the potential durability and flexibility of Chinese Communist culture.

For instance, although the regime has periodically furthered a myth of total severance from the traditional past, and especially so during the Cultural Revolution, its rhetoric of reform and style of rectitude suggest that it carries that condemned Confucian past in its bones. This very inconsistency between official claim and psychic actuality becomes a source of strength because it means retention of sustaining elements of continuity. Similarly, the regime's inability to seal the country off fully from contemporary historical (especially "revisionist") influences becomes in the long run a source of viability, though the degree of isolation achieved does present very serious problems. Perhaps the real test for Chinese Communist culture will lie in the not too distant future when it confronts the full impact of international influence and has to deal with its own developing version of protean man—a test Russia has been facing for some time. Nor should one assume the absolute impossibility of some kind of *modus vivendi* between the regime and a protean style emerging among certain groups of its people.

Concerning the violation of the young and the interruption of their educational process, we may anticipate profound reverberations. But any estimate of the situation must also take into account the special malleability of the young. This malleability falls considerably short of what Maoists have often assumed it to be, but it may well be sufficient to enable many to surrender their militant rectitude with a mixture of disillusionment and relief, and to sustain in their own fashion the loss of their schooling. And if we assume that China's young have already absorbed a certain amount of the protean style, this would further enhance their psychological capacity to "move on" from the Dionysian interlude of the Cultural Revolution to the somewhat more prosaic life-styles likely to emerge in post-Maoist Chinese society. In the long run such protean tendencies, among organizers as well as organized, could enable the society to make use of residual Maoist influences in new and experimental combinations. There is perhaps a hint of this in an evolving form of "progressive education" which seems to contain elements reminiscent not only of Marx, Lenin, and Mao, but also of John

Dewey.* And when talking about "youth," one forgets too easily the new start made possible by the rhythms of generations—the periodic emergence of large numbers of young adults who have as yet experienced neither revolutionary exultation nor disillusionment and who can be drawn anew into national programs of development or revitalization.

When we speak of problems of authority and abuse of the shame sanction, we raise vast issues that will require a great deal more time to evaluate. The regime, to be sure, has never before taken such liberties either with its own structure of authority or with the use (and abuse) of public methods of shaming and humiliation. But one must also consider its well-established pattern of social manipulation: the periodic campaigns and mass movements of extraordinary scope, carved out from the time of the Communist takeover in 1949 and based upon models established well before then. The Chinese themselves refer to this pattern as "unity-struggle-unity." It consists of the interruption of relative social calm with a highly organized explosion of accusations of impurity and a great wave of criticism, self-criticism, and confession—followed in turn by some form of resolution and return to stability. The

* I refer to the stress upon a policy of learning by doing, the "half-work, half-study" system, which apparently had its origins in Yenan and was greatly emphasized during the Cultural Revolution.[3] This "half-half" system cannot be said to derive from any direct influence of John Dewey—though such influence could be making itself indirectly felt, given the great impact of Dewey's ideas (originating from the American philosopher's famous lecture tour throughout China in 1919–1920) upon the generation to which present senior leaders belong.

Cultural Revolution has followed this model, however unprecedented in violence its stage of "struggle" has been. The point at issue now is the degree to which the third stage—the return to stability—can be "managed" by the regime, and the degree to which a measure of political and psychological unity can be re-established. To the extent that it can, emotions of guilt and shame can be put back into some balance with general social policies and goals. If not, they will contribute to every kind of dislocation, every form of anxiety and rage. What one can say is that there is at least a precedent for recovery from induced struggle, if not from the kind of induced catastrophe of the Cultural Revolution.*

With the psychological idiom we have been using the great imponderable is the degree to which a post-Cultural Revolution regime can hold out to the Chinese people a form of symbolic immortality less extreme, and less dependent upon psychism, than that so recently put forward by Mao. We would expect a vision of revolutionary immortality to remain important, but possibly in more open

---

* This pattern of unity-struggle-unity is also, in a more general way, consistent with cyclic imagery deeply ingrained in traditional Chinese philosophical and historical thought. It is epitomized by the famous first line of the *Romance of the Three Kingdoms,* which in the past educated Chinese have almost always been able to recite verbatim: "Empires wax and wane; states cleave asunder and coalesce." The concept is said to go back to the great historian Ssuma Ch'ien (145–86 B.C.). And the quality of the officials of a particular regime has often been viewed as the controlling factor in the timing of these cycles of order and disorder—as revealed by the comment (quoted earlier) of the nineteenth-century educator-official: ". . . as the mind dominates nature, so the quality of officials decides the fate of the Empire."

combination with new forms and other modes—biological, creative, theological, natural, and experiential. Meanwhile, we may expect that the Cultural Revolution will leave its traumatic impact in more ways than can now be imagined. Yet I believe it would be very rash to assume that a regime which has so recently commanded so much psychic power would suddenly cease to possess any at all.

It is in the nature of great men and great revolutions to be dissatisfied with their accomplishments, however extraordinary, and to plunge into realms even they cannot conquer. If this be the meaning of tragedy, the tragedy is not merely theirs. Nor is the present task of recovering from Mao's excesses—and evolving an equilibrium between life and death appropriate to our age—that of China alone.

SOURCE NOTES

I (pp. 6–8)

1. Benjamin Schwartz ("Upheaval in China," *Commentary,* February, 1967, pp. 55–62) emphasizes Mao's "nostalgic idealization" of the "idyllic days of Yenan," as does Mark Gayn ("China Convulsed," *Foreign Affairs,* January, 1967, pp. 246–259), who, to the best of my knowledge, first used the terms "Yenan syndrome" and "Yenan complex." Franz Schurmann ("What Is Happening in China?" *New York Review,* October 20, 1966, pp. 18–25, and January 12, 1967, pp. 32–35) speaks of Mao's anticipation, on the basis of American escalation of the Vietnam war, of an impending "moment of confrontation" with America. Joseph Levenson ("An Exchange on China," *New York Review,* January 12, 1967, pp. 31–32) describes "a conviction of present crisis," which renders "the pastness of the past . . . not so certain, because the future is so uncertain." And Martin Bernal ("Puritanism Chinese-Style," *New York Review,* October 26, 1967, pp. 23–27) sees the Cultural Revolution as a "temporary break between the two forces that have created the Chinese Revolution: 'catholic' and 'protestant,' organization and inspiration." These writings are consistent with different aspects of the point of view I shall set forth, as is Roderick MacFarquar's "Mao's Last Revolution" (*Foreign Affairs,* October, 1966, pp. 112–124), though only Schurmann's and Levenson's articles were available to me when I originally prepared my manuscript. See also writings by Father L. LaDany ("Mao's China: The Decline of a Dynasty," *Foreign Affairs,* July, 1967, pp. 610–623, and the continuing commentary in *China News Analysis,* which Father LaDany edits from Hong Kong); Gene T. Hsiao ("The Background and Development of the

Proletarian Cultural Revolution," *Asian Survey*, June, 1967, pp. 389–404); H. C. Chuang ("The Great Proletarian Cultural Revolution: A Terminological Study," Berkeley, Calif.: Center for Chinese Studies, Studies in Chinese Communist Terminology, No. 12); Michael Oksenberg ("China: Forcing the Revolution to a New Stage," *Asian Survey*, January, 1967, pp. 1–15); and Robert Elegant ("China's Next Phase," *Foreign Affairs*, October, 1967, pp. 137–150).

When this book was in press I came upon Gouldner's and Horowitz' "The Red Guard" (*Trans-Action*, November, 1966), whose sociological interpretation is similar to my own psychohistorical one. I also made extensive use of translations and summaries of Chinese Communist newspapers and periodicals, and of the "great-character posters" of Red Guards and other groups. The latter, which were especially prominent during the early days of the Cultural Revolution as daily commentaries (unofficial but significant) on directions of thought and action, appeared at various focal points in the large cities; they were consistent with the use of "wall newspapers" in earlier Chinese Communist campaigns. Translations appeared in *Survey of China Mainland Press* and selections from *China Mainland Magazine*, both published by the American Consulate General in Hong Kong; in *China News Analysis;* and in newspaper articles in *The New York Times, The Times* and *The Observer* (London), and *The Guardian* (Manchester). I also availed myself of the extensive coverage in the Japanese press; and of the various Eastern and Western European commentaries appearing in American, British, and Japanese publications. Direct quotations of Chinese writings, unless otherwise identified, come from one of these sources. Also very useful were a number of commentaries appearing in *Current Scene* (published by the American Consulate General in Hong Kong), in the *China Quarterly* (London), and in *Asian Survey* (Berkeley, Calif.).

2. See my *Death in Life: Suvivors of Hiroshima* (New York: Random House, 1968); and "On Death and Death Symbolism: The Hiroshima Disaster, *Psychiatry* (1964) 27:191–208. In a forthcoming study, *The Broken Connection,* I elaborate on the theory of symbolic immortality and apply it to a variety of individual and historical situations.

II (*pp. 11–14*)

1. The interview was held on January 9, 1965. See Edgar Snow, "Interview with Mao, *The New Republic,* February 27, 1965, in Franz Schurmann and Orville Schell, *The China Reader; Vol. III: Communist China* (New York: Random House and Vintage Books, 1966, 1967), pp. 359–375.
2. *Death in Life,* Chapter XII.

III (*p. 24*)

1. Hsiao, p. 395.

IV (*pp. 31–41*)

1. Clifford Geertz, "The Impact of the Concept of Culture on the Concept of Man, *Bulletin of the Atomic Scientists,* April, 1966, p. 6.
2. I introduce these concepts of victimization, and contending modes of immortality, in *Death in Life* and discuss them more extensively in *The Broken Connection.* Concerning the language of the Cultural Revolution, see Chuang.
3. Maurice Meisner, "Utopian Goals and Ascetic Values in Chinese Communist Ideology," *Journal of Asian Studies,* in press.

V (*pp. 46–60*)

1. C. P. Fitzgerald, *China: A Short Cultural History* (London: The Cresset Press, 1954 revision), pp. 75–76.
2. R. J. Lifton, *Thought Reform and the Psychology of Totalism: A Study of "Brainwashing" in China* (New York: Norton Library [paperback], 1963), pp. 433–435.
3. Robert A. Burton of the University of Kansas was one of the first observers to emphasize the significance of the Paris Commune for the Cultural Revolution. I am indebted to him for discussions of the question in Hong Kong, and for his making available to me a memo he had prepared on the subject in which the phrase quoted from Marx appeared.
4. *Peking Review,* February 17, 1967, p. 5.
5. Chalmers Johnson, "Lin Piao's Army and Its Role in Chinese Society," Part II, *Current Scene,* July 15, 1966, pp. 9, 1. See also

Alexander L. George, *The Chinese Communist Army in Action* (New York: Columbia, 1967).

6. See *Thought Reform*, pp. 390–393.

VI (*pp. 63–97*)

1. Paper presented to Seminar on East Asian Thought and Society at Stanford University, November 21, 1957, mimeographed.

2. Marcel Granet, *Chinese Civilization* (London: Routledge & Kegan Paul, 1930), p. 313.

3. Arthur F. Wright, "The Chinese Language and Foreign Ideas," in Wright (ed.), *Studies in Chinese Thought* (Chicago: University of Chicago Press, 1953), pp. 286–303.

4. I have used the official English translation, published by The Foreign Languages Press, Peking, 1966. Additional quotations from Mao in this and subsequent chapters are from *Selected Works of Mao Tse-tung*, either the London (Lawrence & Wishart, 1954) or the Peking (Foreign Languages Press, 1965–1967) edition; and from Stuart Schram's excellent recent biography *Mao Tse-tung* (London: Penguin [Pelican], 1966). Other invaluable background works are Schram's *The Political Thought of Mao Tse-tung* (New York: Frederick A. Praeger, 1963); Franz Schurmann, *Ideology and Organization in Communist China* (Berkeley: University of California Press, 1966); Benjamin Schwartz, *Chinese Communism and the Rise of Mao* (Cambridge: Harvard University Press, 1951); C. Brandt, B. Schwartz, and J. Fairbank, *A Documentary History of Chinese Communism* (Cambridge: Harvard University Press, 1951); Jerome Ch'en, *Mao and the Chinese Revolution* (New York: Oxford University Press, 1965); Schurmann and Schell, *The China Reader; Vol. III: Communist China;* John Wilson Lewis, *Leadership in Communist China* (Ithaca: Cornell University Press, 1963); and that still fundamental source book on Mao, Edgar Snow's *Red Star Over China* (London: Victor Gollancz, 1937). In all cases I have retained the rendering of Chinese names used by the translator, even where these do not follow current practice.

5. *Idealogy and Organization*, pp. 29, 17–104.

6. Parton Keese, "More Pong than Ping," *The New York Times Magazine*, October 22, 1967, p. 149.

7. *Death in Life*, Chapter VI, and pp. 481–482; *The Broken Connection*.

8. Lin Mo-han, *Raise Higher the Banner of Mao Tse-tung's Thought on Art and Literature* (Peking: The Foreign Languages Press, 1961), pp. 27, 28. Kuo Mo-jo was probably the first to use the term "revolutionary romanticism" in an article he wrote in *Hung ch'i* (No. 3) in 1958.

9. *Mao Tse-tung*, p. 293. The quotation concerning Mao in the previous sentence, also taken from Schram's biography (p. 253), is originally from Tso Shun-sheng, *Interesting Events in the Past Thirty Years*.

10. *Red Star Over China*, pp. 80, 81.

11. *Ibid.*, p. 83.

12. From an interview with Agnes Smedley, as quoted in Schram, *Mao Tse-tung*, p. 201.

13. Mark Gayn, "Mao Tse-tung Reassessed," in Schurmann and Schell, pp. 92–108, 104–105.

14. Schram, *Mao Tse-tung*, p. 352. All of the poems I quote are Schram's translations or adaptations, as appearing in his biography of Mao. The official interpretations referred to are from the same volume, and Schram adds his own perceptive views.

15. "Interview with Mao," p. 370.

16. *Death in Life*, pp. 512–514, and general section on the survivor, pp. 479–541.

17. I evolved these comparisons of Mao and Gandhi from discussions of both men during the 1967 meeting of the Group for the Study of Psychohistorical Process, and am indebted to Erik Erikson for his presentation of relevant material from his forthcoming study on Gandhi.

18. The text reference to the "rickety bookcase" and its contents is from "Mao Tse-tung Reassessed," p. 94. (The Communists evacuated Yenan shortly after Gayn's visit, and it is possible that preparations for the evacuation had rendered conditions even more primitive than they previously had been.) Other references are: Gunther Stein, *The Challenge of Red China* (New York: McGraw-Hill, 1945), pp. 107–108; Evans F. Carlson, *Twin Stars of China* (New

York: Dodd, Mead, 1940), pp. 166–167; and "Upheaval in China," p. 56.

19. *Mao Tse-tung*, p. 329.

VII (*pp. 103–122*)

1. Schurmann and Schell, pp. 401–402.

2. Kang Chao, "The Great Leap," in *ibid.*, pp. 407–416, 408.

3. "Mao Tse-tung Reassessed," p. 103.

4. The term is Schram's, characterizing the poem, which is reproduced in his *Mao Tse-tung*, p. 209.

5. "The Great Leap," p. 416.

6. Schram, *Mao Tse-tung*, p. 294.

7. Mary C. Wright, *The Last Stand of Chinese Conservatism: The T'ung-chih Restoration, 1862–1874* (New York: Atheneum, 1966; paperback); see especially pp. 91–95, 43, 68–69, and 244–245.

8. Quoted in *Mao Tse-tung*, p. 295. (Italics mine.)

9. Derk Bodde, *Peking Diary*, in Schurmann and Schell, p. 13.

10. "Mao Tse-tung Reassessed," p. 99.

11. K. Mendelssohn, "Science in China," *Nature* (1967) 215:10–12.

12. See Jonathan Spence, "On Chinese Revolutionary Literature," *Yale French Studies*, issue on Literature and Revolution, No. 39, 1967, 215–225.

13. Robert Havemann, *Dialektik oder dogma?* (Berlin, 1964), as quoted in Edmund Demaitre, "In Search of Humanism," *Problems of Communism*, September–October, 1965, pp. 18–30, 29.

14. For more detailed discussions of China's relationship to nuclear weapons, see Morton H. Halperin, *China and the Bomb* (New York: Frederick A. Praeger, 1965), and the same author's two-part study "China and Nuclear Proliferation," in the November and December, 1966, issues of the *Bulletin of the Atomic Scientists;* Alice Langley Shieh, *Communist China's Strategy in the Nuclear Era* (Englewood Cliffs, N.J.: Prentice-Hall, 1962), and *The Sino-Soviet Nuclear Dialogue*, RAND p–2852 (1963); Oran R. Young, "Chinese Views on the Spread of Nuclear Weapons," *China Quarterly*, November–December, 1966, pp. 136–170; and Ralph L. Powell, "Great

Powers and Atomic Bombs are 'Paper Tigers,' " *China Quarterly*, July–September, 1965, pp. 55–63.

15. "Mao Tse-tung Reassessed," pp. 106–107.

16. *Long Live Leninism!* (Peking: The Foreign Languages Press, 1960), p. 22, quoted in *Mao Tse-tung*, p. 302. Other uncited quotations in this section from and about Mao can also be found in Schram's volume.

17. "Interview with Mao," p. 365.

18. Quotations in this sentence are from the *People's Daily* (Peking) and *Peking Review*, October, 1964, and can be found in Powell, p. 59.

19. See writings of Halperin and Young, note 14 *supra*.

20. Powell, p. 61.

21. Stanley Karnow, in Washington Post Service dispatch, *New Haven Register*, October 26, 1967.

22. S. Chandrasekhar, "Marx, Malthus and Mao: China's Population Explosion," *Current Scene*, February 28, 1967. Much of the discussion that follows is based on this article.

VIII (pp. 129–144)

1. *Thought Reform*, pp. 410–415.

2. *Wen Hui Pao*, July 10, 1967, quoted in F. T. Mits, "The Wanderers," *Current Scene*, August 15, 1967, pp. 1–7, 2. Subsequent quotations about wanderers are from the same source. And the reference to Taoist mysticism is also from Mits.

3. *China News Analysis*, October 6, 1967.

4. Various aspects of the phenomenon of charisma that are consistent with my discussion here have been emphasized by Edward Shils ("Charisma, Order, and Status"; mimeographed); Robert C. Tucker ("The Theory of Charismatic Leadership," *Daedalus*, in press); and David E. Apter ("Nkrumah, Charisma, and the Coup," *Daedalus*, in press).

5. R. J. Lifton, "Individual Patterns in Historical Change: Imagery of Japanese Youth," *Disorders of Communication: Association for Research in Nervous and Mental Disease*, Vol. XLII (1964), 291–306,

reprinted in *Comparative Studies in Society and History* (1964) 4:369–383. The discussion of restorationism and transformationism that follows is based on ideas expressed in this article.

6. See D. W. Fokkema, "Chinese Criticism of Humanism: Campaigns Against the Intellectuals 1964–1965," *China Quarterly*, April–June, 1966, pp. 68–81, 76–78, from which quotations in this paragraph are taken. See also Donald J. Munro, "Dissent in Communist China: The Current Anti-Intellectual Campaign in Perspective," *Current Scene*, June 1, 1966; and Merle Goldman, *Literary Dissent in Communist China* (Cambridge: Harvard University Press, 1967).

7. *China News Analysis*, November 3, 1967.

8. Harold Kahn and Albert Feuerwerker, "The Ideology of Scholarship: China's New Historiography," *China Quarterly*, April–June, 1965, pp. 1–13, 1, 4.

IX (*pp. 152–159*)

1. R. J. Lifton, "Protean Man," *Partisan Review*, Winter, 1968, pp. 13–27.

2. The discussion that follows owes much to questions raised by Arthur Wright during a highly informative presentation on the Cultural Revolution and its Chinese context to the Collegium on the Future, at Yale University, October 31, 1967.

3. See Donald J. Munro, "Maxims and Realities in China's Educational Policy: The Half-Work, Half-Study Model," *Asian Survey*, April, 1967, pp. 254–272.

Index

About the Author

ROBERT JAY LIFTON holds the Foundation's Fund for Research in Psychiatry professorship at Yale University. He has been particularly interested in the relationship between individual psychology and historical change, especially in China and Japan, and in problems surrounding the extreme historical situations in our era. He has spent almost seven years in the Far East, including an extensive stay from 1960 to 1962, during which he carried out a study of psychological patterns in Japanese youth as well as an investigation of the psychological effects of the atomic bomb in Hiroshima. He has recently returned from another Far Eastern trip devoted to follow-up work in Japan and to an evaluation of current trends in mainland China.

Dr. Lifton was born in New York City in 1926 and received his medical degree from New York Medical College. From 1956 to 1961 he was Research Associate in Psychiatry at Harvard, where he was also affiliated with the Center for East Asian Studies; prior to that he was a member of the faculty of the Washington School of Psychiatry. He lives in Woodbridge, Connecticut, with his wife, a writer, and their two small children.

He is the author of *Death in Life: Survivors of Hiroshima, Thought Reform and the Psychology of Totalism: A Study of "Brainwashing" in China,* and the editor of *The Woman in America.* In addition, his writings have appeared in *Partisan Review, American Scholar,* and the *New Republic,* as well as in South Asian journals and in various psychiatric and psychological journals.